"Clear, biblical, and personal, *You Are God's Plan A* is a must-read for anyone seeking God's purpose for their lives."

Eric Affeldt, president and CEO of ClubCorp

"With authenticity and transparency, Dwight Robertson delivers the message that all God's followers are uniquely called to ministry. Regardless of our vocation, a fulfilled life is loving and serving others in Christ. *You Are God's Plan A* is a call to action. It encourages and empowers the personal ministry of loving individually and caring deeply."

W. Ralph Jones III, president and CEO of Jones Companies, Ltd.

"Dwight Robertson's *You Are God's Plan A* is a riveting book that gives permission to every Christian to live an unashamed, victorious life for Christ our King. This book helps us to know that everyone is a minister and the ministry looks like our lives. God purposefully gave each of us gifts, and this book inspires us to use them for the building of the Kingdom!"

Adrian Despres Jr., evangelist and chaplain of University of South Carolina football

"Dwight Robertson's book *You Are God's Plan A* is powerful! It hits a chord in every one of us, no matter where we are in life. In the end, the only important question will be 'What difference did my life make?' And the only appraisal that will matter is what God thinks. This book is a Spirit-anointed guide that will assist you in your personal journey."

C. Kemmons Wilson Jr., founding family of Holiday Inn

"Dwight Robertson has produced a page-turning, Kingdom-advancing, great read. *You Are God's Plan A* is filled with chance encounters, God's little coincidences, divine appointments, and holy disturbances. These define Dwight's life, and they describe a life committed to God's Plan A. Are they occurring in your life?"

Joyce Godwin, former board chair of ECFA, ISI, MAF, and AirServ International

"If you have ever wrestled with questions like 'Can God use me?' or 'Could I really make an eternal difference?'—and all of us have—this practical and powerfully illustrated book gives a resounding *yes*! Dwight Robertson makes a compelling case answering both why and how every believer should get 'off the sidelines and in the game.' This book is on my must-read list; I highly recommend it to you!"

Steve Moore, president of Mission Exchange, founder of Keep Growing, Inc., and author of *The Dream Cycle: Leveraging the Power of Personal Growth*

"*You Are God's Plan A* is an absolute encouragement to me because it loudly declares that everyday people are the ones God will use to transform the planet. We just have to look at life through God's lens. This book is a reminder that changing the world is not about

What people are saying about …

You Are God's Plan A

"Understanding the unique and powerful plan of God for our lives ushers in a sense of dignity, purpose, courage, compassion, and strength that God alone can construct. Dwight Robertson splashes light across a confused and cluttered subject. He reconnects us to The Plan … in fact, God's Plan for each of us, and in doing so he ignites our soul. From the scrap heap of do-it-yourself, Dwight draws us back to the beauty of God's initial design and Plan. This is why He made us … this is where we find our ultimate joy."

Dan Wolgemuth, president and
CEO of Youth for Christ/USA

"Dwight Robertson expresses on paper what overflows out of his heart: an intense passion for the vehicle God uses to draw people into His Kingdom—laborers! By the time you complete this book, you'll have caught the same zeal to use your ordinary gifts and abilities, while also allowing and expecting God to come through in extraordinary ways."

Bay Forest, former Phoenix Suns NBA player,
speaker, author, and founder of Focus Ministries

"Every once in a while you get exposed to a concept so potent it changes the way you see the world. *You Are God's Plan A* was one of those concepts for me. I was first introduced to this message as a college student. It has followed me, remained in me, and shaped my ministry for the last decade. Dwight was the first person who clearly explained to me that every ordinary life can make an extraordinary difference for the kingdom of God. The awareness of this reality has served me well and enabled me to empower thousands of others. I am now the pastor of a church that grew from 0 to more than 5,000 over the course of a few short years. The paradigm that facilitated this kind of explosive growth all goes back to a simple and powerful message I heard in college: *You Are God's Plan A.*"

Steven Furtick, lead pastor of Elevation Church

"Dwight Robertson speaks to the *every* in *every*one of us. *Every* part of us. *Every* bit of us. *Every* element of us. With practical power, he encourages us to both embrace and invest all God has made us to be for His Kingdom purposes."

Elisa Morgan, president emerita of MOPS, publisher of *FullFill*™, and author of *She Did What She Could*

"Every believer needs to know that they have been 'fearfully and wonderfully made'—with gifting and an assignment as a builder in the Kingdom of God. Dwight is an anointed speaker and writer who captures the essence of this profound truth in this discourse. This book is a must-read for preacher, elder, deacon, praise team, and parishioner."

Raleigh Washington, DD,
president of Promise Keepers

having a position, but a disposition … to give our lives. Get ready to be challenged by the stories in this book."

Dr. Tim Elmore, founding president of Growing Leaders and author of *Habitudes*

"The call of *You Are God's Plan A* is clear and concise. In the mind of God, there is only one option and that option is us! As a pastor, I can only imagine what would happen if the people of God lived out the words of this book. If we answer the call, we will see the Lord transform the way we view our lives and the people around us."

Robert Gelinas, lead pastor of Colorado Community Church and author of *Finding the Groove*

"*You Are God's Plan A* is filled with fresh, thought-provoking life experiences that will help you find and connect with the purpose God has shaped for you. More than ever, I've been encouraged to 'get off the sidelines' and get involved in God's Plan A for reaching the world."

Georg Andersen, ASID, architectural/interior designer, and author of *Silent Witness*

"God is waiting to bless you and challenge you through the prayerful reading of this book. Let Him speak to you, guide you, and use you mightily. God wants to fill you with Himself and make you a vital part of His Plan A."

Dr. Wesley L. Duewel, president emeritus of OMS International, and author of *Mighty Prevailing Prayer*

"CAUTION: Do not read this book if your desire is to be a spectator in the Kingdom of God. This book will challenge and change you … but equally important, it will leave you encouraged."

Tobin Cassels III, president of
Southeastern Freight Lines

"Dwight Robertson's book *You Are God's Plan A* masterfully shows that every life matters. It proves that God gives all of us (who are ordinary people) the opportunity to impact the world beyond our imagination."

Ryan DeVoe, founding family of
JD Byrider Corporation

"I highly recommend this book to anyone who wants to live a life of purpose. *You Are God's Plan A* changed the way I look at living life and will bring transformation of thought and actions to anyone who reads it."

Scott Porter, president of Formula Boats

"This is a book of encouragement that every Christian needs to read. Read it, then pass it on."

Bill English, author and
consultant for Mindsharp

YOU ARE GOD'S Plan A

{and there is no plan b}

Dwight Robertson

YOU ARE GOD'S PLAN A
Published by David C. Cook
4050 Lee Vance View
Colorado Springs, CO 80918 U.S.A.

David C. Cook Distribution Canada
55 Woodslee Avenue, Paris, Ontario, Canada N3L 3E5

David C. Cook U.K., Kingsway Communications
Eastbourne, East Sussex BN23 6NT, England

The stories presented in this book are personal and include details about the lives of family members, friends, and neighbors. While some names and story details have been changed for privacy's sake, I've sought to remain true to the essence and impact of each story.

LCCN 2009940961
ISBN 978-1-4347-6463-8
eISBN 978-1-4347-0189-3

Published in association with the literary agency of Wolgemuth & Associates, Inc.
First edition published by Kingdom Building Ministries in 2006

The Team: John Blase, Susan Tjaden, Amy Kiechlin,
Sarah Schultz, Jack Campbell, and Karen Athen
Cover Concept: Brand Innovation Group
Cover Design: Amy Kiechlin
Cover Photo: iStockphoto

Printed in the United States of America
Second Edition 2010

2 3 4 5 6 7 8 9 10 11

051410

Discover More Online

Study questions available at

www.DavidCCook.com/PlanA

Contents

Foreword

We are living in an ever-increasing multiethnic, multicultural, and urbanized world. Technology has also given us access to a fast-paced and global perspective on this challenging and complex reality. For Christians today the cultural realities surrounding us can seem somewhat intimidating. We may wonder, *How can I advance the Kingdom of God within all of this?* or, *Do I really have what it takes to make a difference in the world?* We may be asking these questions of ourselves, while at the same time wrestling with an inner desire to find our God-created purpose.

It seems that it was not too long ago that just about everyone went to church. And, for the most part, those I went to church with and lived in community with appeared to look the same and share the same values. Well, a lot has changed in what seems to have been a relatively short period of time. Many church researchers are saying that on any given Sunday less than 30 percent of those living in the United States are in church. Many Christian sociologists are saying that even though our nation is becoming more and more multicultural, the church is still the most racially segregated institution we have. These two issues alone pose a great challenge for the body of Christ.

Even in the midst of these and other challenges, there is great news revealed in this book. God is not intimidated by the realities existing within the world He created. No matter the complexities, God is still in the business of using ordinary people to be about the extraordinary work of Kingdom advancement in the earth. Yes, God has decided to use you and me—no matter what is going on in the world—to be vehicles of His love, truth, compassion, mercy, justice, and transformation. The words in the opening chapter of the book of Jeremiah ring true for us today: Before we were formed in our mothers' wombs, God knew us and set us apart for an incredible work. This is what God unfolds through Dwight Robertson in this book. God has placed a Plan A within each and every one of us, that we might participate in the revolution of His Kingdom being made manifest on the earth.

We cannot do this work in our own power. Only through the death and resurrection of Jesus Christ and the indwelling of the Holy Spirit are we equipped for what Dwight Robertson calls "laborership." This dear brother and friend is the leading voice on equipping the laity of the church in finding their personal, God-breathed, Kingdom-building ministry. Yes, there are many challenges facing us today, but we can be Kingdom laborers and radical reconcilers expressing the love of God in the world. This passionate and practical resource, I believe, is a vital tool for the empowerment of an army of laborers prepared to advance the Kingdom of God right where they are.

Efrem Smith, senior pastor of
the Sanctuary Covenant Church,
author of *Raising Up Young Heroes,* and
coauthor of *The Hip-Hop Church*

Introduction

Over many years, evangelist Billy Graham has earned respect from people of all faiths. But during the cold war era, at the height of the Brezhnev regime, he faced quite a bit of ridicule from conservatives in America for visiting the Soviet Union and meeting with leaders from the government and state church. "Why would Dr. Graham treat the enemies of America and detractors of the Western church with such courtesy and respect? Shouldn't he condemn Soviet human-rights abuses and their restraints on religious liberty?" they scoffed. One critic blamed him for setting the church back fifty years.

Upon hearing the accusation, Graham lowered his head and answered, "I am deeply ashamed. I have been trying very hard to set the church back *two thousand* years."

God's Plan A for redeeming the world was enacted two thousand years ago. But don't take that to mean the plan is irrelevant or outdated. God's plan is as relevant, powerful, and doable today as it was when Jesus enacted it.

But somehow over time, people have diluted, distorted, and even forgotten His plan. In order to understand it, then, we must press the rewind button and go back two thousand years to the days when Jesus walked the earth.

Really Seeing People

When I read the gospel accounts of Jesus' life and envision how He lived and ministered to the people around Him, I'm struck by the contrast to how most of us live our lives and approach ministry today.

When Jesus saw people, He didn't hurry past them—without noticing them—in order to get to His next meeting at the synagogue. He noticed people and their needs. He acknowledged them by slowing down and connecting with them in life-giving ways. He *saw* them and *stopped,* becoming God's extended plan of love and grace to those in need.

> Jesus went about all the cities and villages, teaching in their synagogues and preaching the gospel of the kingdom, and healing every disease and every infirmity. When he saw the crowds, he had compassion for them, because they were harassed and helpless, like sheep without a shepherd. (Matthew 9:35–36 RSV)

When people in Jesus' day used the word *saw,* they understood it meant not only seeing with the eyes but also perceiving and seeing below the surface to a person's thoughts and heart—to the person's true self. In fact, in Jesus' day, the distinction between seeing people on the surface and seeing people below the surface didn't exist. So this Scripture passage and others like it tell us that when Jesus saw the people around Him, He truly *saw* them, through and through.

Most of us don't. Not really.

"I See You!"

Not long ago, my son, Dreyson, started the school year at a new elementary school. When he returned home after the first day, I asked him how his day had gone.

"Awful, Dad," he moaned. "All the other kids already have their friends. They didn't even notice me. No one saw me at recess. No one sat by me in the school cafeteria. And no one talked to me in class or after school. I was *invisible,* Dad!"

An interesting word choice, isn't it? And yet, unfortunately, *many* people feel this same way. Every day they live overlooked, unnoticed, and unseen lives. "Invisible" seems to best express how they feel.

How often do we see people with our eyes but fail to see them past the surface? We may see them according to a category we've created for them or the role they play in our lives, but we often fail to discover anything else about them. *Seeing* a person as more than your neighbor—or the kid next door whose parents work all the time, or the guy in the cubicle next to you, or the checkout girl who bags your groceries—isn't easy. But none of those people should be categorized. They're real people with real lives and real stories. Unfortunately, most of us spend little time interacting with them. We barely even get to know their names, let alone any of the details of their lives.

It's time we slowed down and started seeing people like Jesus did. Or like people from the Zulu tribe in southern Africa do. Zulus greet each other by saying "I *see* you!" The response is "I am here!" What a powerful greeting!

The moments you share with people are more than transactions—they're interactions. Do your actions say "I see you!" to the people around you? The change is subtle yet significant. Next time people serve you at a restaurant, bank, or store, speak to them as if you truly see them. Instead of responding to them as if they were impersonal servants, treat them like real people with real lives and real stories. Now, that may not seem like a big deal to you, but it will be to them.

Greet your servers by name (they usually wear a name tag) and ask them about their day. Encourage them. Tell them what you appreciate about their service. When you do, you'll be among the very few who *see* them.

And you'll be setting the church back two thousand years.

Beyond Seeing

Seeing is important. But Jesus didn't just see people. He *stopped* and served them. Seeing and stopping were two of the recurring hallmarks of His love.

He looked into the faces of children who weren't highly valued in society … and He stopped; He made the time to hold them on His lap.

When a man covered with leprosy fell to his knees and begged Jesus, "Lord, if you are willing, you can make me clean," Jesus *stopped* and touched him (Luke 5:12–13).

When He encountered a woman caught in adultery, He *stopped* and called her to a better life (John 8:1–11).

When faced with people oppressed and tormented by evil spirits, He *stopped* and delivered them (Matthew 8:28–34, for example).

When He encountered Matthew in his workplace, He *stopped* and began a long-term relationship with him (Matthew 9:9).

When everyone else ignored and walked past hurting people, Jesus didn't. He saw them and stopped.

Jesus never knew a stranger. Everyone belonged in one category: people to love. He valued others by asking them questions, discerning their needs, touching them, and serving them in practical ways. Every changed life resulted from an engaging conversation with a stranger.

In the same way, we can follow in Jesus' footsteps by engaging strangers with a smile, an open heart, a word of encouragement, or even a spiritual deposit that could potentially change a life.

One Word

At one point, Jesus turned to His disciples and shared *with them one word* that explained why He stopped and saw in response to the needs around Him:

> Then [Jesus] said to his disciples, "The harvest is plentiful, but the *laborers* are few; pray therefore the Lord of the harvest to send out *laborers* into his harvest." (Matthew 9:37–38 RSV)

The word? *Laborers.*

It may not be a very glamorous word, yet it's what will set us back two thousand years to the way Jesus lived and ministered—and move us forward into a bright future, building God's Kingdom according to His Plan A. What the world needs, Jesus said, are laborers. Common, everyday laborers.

Laborers are Jesus' means for reaching the world with His love and forgiveness. They aren't just critical to His plan. They *are* His plan.

His only plan.

Kingdom *laborers* are God's Plan A.

But what exactly is a laborer? After all, it's not a normal household word people use to describe most Christians. After studying the word in Scripture, I've developed a simple definition: *Laborers are ordinary people who deeply love God and actively love others. They seek to live a life of love ... every moment of every day.*

A laborer is a minister—not just the professional kind like pastors and missionaries, but the common, ordinary kind like my wife (an art teacher) and children (students).

Laborers are everyday, everyplace ministers like my friend Shane, who works as a radio executive and leads some of his seeker friends and coworkers in a Tuesday-morning "breakfast club," sharing relevant Bible truth from his own life and helping them better discover God's amazing love and purpose for their lives.

Or like my friend Bill, who owns a large freight company and deeply cares for the welfare of his employees.

Or like my friends Norm and Becky, who served a short stint as overseas missionaries before unexpectedly returning home. They decided God must be sending them into a different kind of ministry. So, Norm pursued a career in sales, and Becky became a full-time mom. And, together, they became "missionaries" in their neighborhood, caring for and sharing with their neighbors in life-changing ways.

Or like James the Roofer, a special guy you will meet in the next chapter.

Laborers are ordinary people who express their love for God through practical, hands-and-feet service. They embody Jesus' primary means for reaching the world with His love. Because they live everyday lives in everyday society, they influence people in ways that few professional ministers could. And through their everyday jobs, they reach people who would never step foot in a church building.

Want to know what a laborer looks like? Look in the mirror. God has called *you* to be one.

And since laborers are God's Plan A for reaching the world, that means *you* are God's Plan A for reaching the world around you.

You are God's Plan A to the other soccer moms and dads you meet when you take your kids to practices and games.

You are God's Plan A to your coworkers, with whom you spend more hours than nearly anyone else.

You are God's Plan A in your neighborhood, where you have time and opportunities to develop natural and meaningful relationships with your neighbors.

You are God's Plan A in your high school classroom or college dorm.

You are God's Plan A at your favorite restaurant, where the servers know your name.

Not your pastor. *You.*

You are God's Plan A. (And did I mention there's no Plan B?)

Part One
THE PLAN

God has a plan

for loving and reaching the world—

it's *you!*

One
Overlooked and Undervalued

"Where did *that* come from?" I asked my wife, Dawn, as I rose from my recliner to take a closer look at the nasty water spot I had just noticed on the entryway ceiling of our home.

"We had some really intense thunderstorms yesterday," she explained, staring at the ugly spot. Apparently the combination of high winds and quarter-sized hail had taken its toll on our roof over the weekend while I was gone.

Dealing with a leaky roof was the last thing I wanted to tackle following a hectic weekend. After a full speaking schedule and then flight delays, missed connections, and turbulence on the way home, I just wanted to relax.

However, when Dawn said another round of storms was forecast to hit that week, I knew the work needed to be done that day. Feeling a bit nervous about hiring someone I knew nothing about—and yet knowing I didn't have much of a choice—I grabbed the Yellow Pages and the phone and started dialing. Seven calls later, I found someone who could fit me into his schedule. When this roofer, James, answered the phone, his reassuring voice and polite manner immediately put me at ease. He told me he could be at my house in four hours.

Right on time, the doorbell rang. Opening the door, I was surprised to see a rugged-looking guy with long hair pulled back in a ponytail. I confess he didn't quite fit the mental image I had conjured up during our phone conversation.

After introducing himself and asking some questions about our problem, he returned to his truck, grabbed his ladder, and climbed up onto the roof to assess the damage. A few minutes later, he crawled back down and quoted me a price for the work. It was surprisingly reasonable. He said the job would take only two or three hours, and he could do it right away. I agreed to the price, and before long, he was back on the roof, making the repair.

About an hour later, I heard a knock on my door. I cringed, thinking it was too soon for him to be done. As I opened the door, I thought to myself, *He's probably going to say that the damage is much worse than he expected—and that it's going to cost a lot more than he quoted.*

"All done!" James announced. "It shouldn't give you any more problems. If it does, just give me a call." Then he handed me a bill at a price that did not match his original quote. It was much *less*.

"I finished your roof quicker than I expected," he said. "So I only charged you for the actual time it took to complete the job."

Thankful for his honesty, I went to my home office to retrieve my checkbook. When I returned, James was talking to another customer on his cell phone. As I wrote out the check, I listened to his interaction with the other person. He treated her with the same professionalism and courtesy as he had treated me.

"Don't ever hire an answering service," I said as I handed him his check. "You really do a great job interacting with your customers on the phone. You have a way of quickly gaining people's confidence."

Then something unexpected happened.

He humbly looked at the ground for a moment, and then he looked me straight in the eyes and said, "Thank you for your kind words, but to be honest, I haven't always been good with people."

"What do you mean?"

"I made some pretty bad choices when I was younger. But about thirteen years ago, God caught my attention, and I began a personal relationship with Him. My life really changed after that. I'm a very different person than I was before."

As he shared some of the changes that had transpired in his life, he occasionally looked down and shook his head, still amazed at the work God had done.

"My desire is to serve God every day by serving my customers with kindness and respect," he explained. "I treat every roofing job as a daily assignment from God."

He spoke so openly about God that I glanced around to see if something had given him a clue that I was also a Christian—like a Bible lying within view. Nothing was there that would tip him off, so I said, "James … brother … hey, I'm a Christian too."

James' face lit up. He was excited to discover that we shared a common faith in God. And I was thrilled to find someone who lived out his faith so naturally in the everyday moments of his work life.

"Do you realize you're going places where few pastors could go and reaching people with your personal story that few pastors could reach?" I asked.

"You know, I've been thinking about that a lot," he replied, "but I've never heard anyone talk about it that way."

"James, God has uniquely positioned you to minister to others!" I continued with a growing sense of excitement. "You remind me of how Jesus ministered when He was here on earth. Most of His ministry took place *outside* the synagogue walls. He met needy people and served them where *they* lived. James, that's what you're doing!"

By that time, Dawn and our two children, Dara and Dreyson, had entered the room. I asked if we could pray for him and his ministry. He agreed, and so our family surrounded James the Roofer and placed our hands on his shoulders.

"Lord," I prayed, "we commission James for ministry. We pray for James just as church leaders would do for missionaries before sending them out to their fields of service."

His body trembled under our hands as we prayed. Then he began sobbing, which I didn't expect from such a rugged guy. Teardrops fell on the hardwood floor, literally forming a small puddle. As we concluded, James needed a moment to regain his composure.

"I'm sorry for crying," he said while sniffling. "It's just that no one has ever treated my ministry as if it's important. For the past thirteen years, I've believed that this is how God has chosen for me to represent Him to others—and in all that time, no one has ever validated that what I do for Him is important."

James went on to explain that he regularly prays that God will send him customers who need to hear about Jesus. Then he prays for each of them by name and asks God to give him opportunities to minister to them. He told us about one of those opportunities:

"A few years ago, I was working on the roof of a home in inner-city Denver. Suddenly a gunshot sounded from inside the house, and then I heard a scream. I scrambled off the roof and ran inside to find an older man lying on the floor in a pool of blood. His family had already called 911, but it was clear the man wasn't going to survive.

"Knowing that this may be his last chance to spend eternity in heaven with Jesus, I knelt down next to him. He couldn't move, but he locked his eyes on me.

"'Sir, God loves you very much. Do you want to know if you're going to be with Him in heaven when you die?' I wasn't sure if the man could hear me. He couldn't talk or move his body, but he could move his eyes up and down as if he were nodding his head. That moment, I led the man into a relationship with Christ by asking him questions and allowing him to continue answering with his eyes. He died a few moments later."

As James finished his story, I looked around at Dawn, Dara, and Dreyson. We were all fighting back tears. Before this holy moment ended, I asked James for his business card and told him I'd place it on our refrigerator next to the other prayer magnets for our missionary friends. Then our family promised James that we would pray for him and his ministry. Although we haven't seen him since that day, we still pray for him.

Then he thanked us repeatedly as he walked out our front door.

After my chance encounter with James the Roofer, I returned to my recliner to reflect on our exchange. God began deeply stirring and convicting my heart. I was grieved because James felt so overlooked and undervalued in his ministry to others. Week after week, he sat in church services that validated "up-front" and "specially called" people in their ministries. But no one had ever validated or commissioned James into the ministry that God had called him.

I thought about the countless people who must feel the same way—the nameless, faceless followers of Jesus who serve Him in ordinary ways in their ordinary lives. But, tragically, no one notices, validates, or affirms their faithfulness. No one notices that their ministries are extremely important to God.

Yet the Bible clearly shows us that God chooses and uses ordinary people like James the Roofer to do the extraordinary work of His Kingdom in the ordinary venues of life.

He always has. He still does. And we have every reason to believe He always will.

Where was it along the way that we lost track of Jesus' plan? When did we become so preoccupied with our own modern methods that we stopped recognizing and valuing the extraordinary work God performs through ordinary people? Instead, we've become enamored with "professional" ministers (people who make a living from their ministry service) and Christian celebrities (the highly gifted few who serve in ministry spotlights and on ministry platforms). We point to these people and methods as the standard for what it means to do something important for God.

But the day-to-day ministry of faithful servants like James the Roofer is at the heart of God's plan for reaching the world.

It's time to take a closer look at what God says in His Word about the nature of ministry and who's called and qualified to do it. Jesus chose the ordinary. He validated the weak. He called out the imperfect. He honored the poor in spirit. He sought after the humble of heart. And He gave them all a significant role to play in His Kingdom work.

If you've avoided involving yourself in the work of God's Kingdom because you don't think you have anything significant to contribute, then I have good news for you: God *wants* to work through you. He *chooses* you.

Perhaps you're like James the Roofer—you faithfully serve God in His Kingdom work, but you feel overlooked, undervalued, and maybe even unimportant. I have good news for you, too: God highly values your service to Him, regardless of the recognition you might receive. His announcement to you right now is "*You* are My plan!"

Two
Wrapped in Ordinary

Grace was about as ordinary as any woman I've ever known. Few people would identify her as a likely candidate for high-impact ministry.

She lived in an old farmhouse on Strawtown Pike in rural Indiana. One of her legs was shorter than the other, giving her a signature limp. In her seventies, Grace wore her wiry gray hair in a bun, along with a colorful dress and nylon stockings that occasionally bunched around her ankles.

Over the years, Grace and her husband raised five boys, all of whom were grown and living with their families in other places. After her husband passed away, she entered a strange season in life—with fewer responsibilities and meaningful things to do.

But Grace didn't want to spend the final years of her life limping to the finish line. She wanted to sprint! So she asked God to give her something significant to do for Him.

"I don't know how God could use an old woman like me, but if He'll show me what He wants me to do, I'll do it!" Grace once told me. God answered her prayers and gave me a front-row seat to watch a miraculous story unfold.

One day, while thumbing through a prison-ministry magazine, she read an open letter from an inmate. Bobby had just committed his life to Christ at a prison revival service, and he wasn't sure what to do next. So in his letter he asked for a "godly grandmother" who would disciple him.

Grace wrote the magazine editor and asked if he could help her get in touch with Bobby. She wanted to be this man's spiritual grandmother. The editor decided to help her.

Grace began by leading Bobby through a Bible study correspondence course. Soon afterward, Bobby led his cellmate to Christ, and he became Grace's second spiritual grandson.

Over lunch a little time later, she showed me pictures of her growing "family" of seven boys—each of whom met Christ through Bobby's influence.

"I'm having the time of my life!" she exclaimed as she recounted their stories.

"Right now, I have a captive audience," she said with a smile and a twinkle in her eye, "but I figure they won't be in prison for the rest of their lives. Today, they'll impact their fellow inmates, but someday, they'll get out of prison and impact the world."

A surprise happened on my next visit. As I walked into her home, I opened her closet door to hang up my coat—but there was no room inside. It was packed with filing cabinets and Bible study booklets. And to my amazement, her couch and coffee table had been replaced by worktables and computers.

"Wow! What's going on, Grace?" I couldn't wait to hear all about it.

"Oh, Dwight, a lot has happened since you were last here," she replied. "God has done more with this ministry than I ever imagined! Did you know that prisoners get transferred? Some of my boys were moved to prisons in Alabama and Texas, and they've been sharing Christ with inmates in those prisons too. I'm now leading Bible studies with inmates in three prisons—all from my little farmhouse on Strawtown Pike."

Impacting the World with Grace

Over the years I have dropped by Grace's house to check up on her. During my last visit, she showed me a world map on her wall with dots all over the Americas.

"Grace, what are all these dots?" I asked.

"Those are my boys and all their 'extras,'" she replied.

"Okay, I know about your boys, but what are their extras?"

"Well, awhile back, some of my boys started getting out of prison, and they'd lead their wives, children, and other family members to Christ. So, they asked me if I'd be a spiritual grandma to their family members as well. Those are the extras that I never expected God to bring into my spiritual family."

"But what about all those dots in the Latin countries?" I asked in amazement. "How did they get there?"

She explained that when some of her Hispanic inmates were released from prison, they introduced her to their friends and family members. Soon, letters written in Spanish started arriving from people in Cuba, so she asked God to send her someone who could translate. God led her to a retired Spanish teacher named Clara.

"I'm in over my head, Dwight!" she chuckled. "We're now discipling more than a thousand Spanish-speaking people, and Clara comes over to my house three days a week to translate their correspondence. I've even added seven college students who volunteer with me."

A few months later, I called her on the phone.

"Grandma Grace, you've been on my mind this week."

"You're not the only one," she quipped with her trademark laugh. "My kids have been thinking about me this week too. In fact, they're worried about me, Dwight. They fear I'm depleting my personal energy, time, and resources beyond the capacity I have to give at this season of life.

"I told them not to worry 'cause souls will be going to heaven!"

Smiling, I asked her a question that had been pestering me for quite some time.

"Grace, how many people are you corresponding with?"

"Oh, that doesn't matter," she said humbly. "I love all of them as if they're my own grandkids."

After some coaxing, she finally answered my question. "I don't know the exact number. Last I counted there were more than ten thousand."

I was shocked. I really didn't know what to say, so she continued as if it were no big deal.

"Last week, the U.S. Postal Service told me I had to get an industrial-sized mailbox or they wouldn't deliver all my mail anymore."

Her eyes twinkled with a bit of mischief as she smiled and said, "Dwight, I have a dream that someday the post office will assign me my own zip code!"

While I chuckled with her about it, my spirit soon gave way to praise. What an amazing feat to witness. God chose to send ripples through all of eternity in the form of an old gray-haired widow who worked out of a farmhouse on Strawtown Pike in rural Indiana.

But this shouldn't come as a surprise. Kingdom multiplication is always God's plan. Throughout history He has often chosen obscure people who live in remote places to accomplish His eternal plans and purposes.

Writer Richard Exley expressed it this way: "God has a history of using the insignificant to accomplish the impossible."

God's Unlikely First-Round Draft Choices

The Bible clearly proves that commonplace laborers aren't the losers who get picked last for God's ministry team while the Christian celebrities get picked first.

Willing laborers are God's first-round draft choices!

Just look at the twelve common men Jesus chose to be His disciples. They weren't superstars or rabbis. No one pointed to them as brilliant scholars or proven leaders. They came from a cross section of average people—small-business owners, an accountant, day laborers, and the like.

In fact, any human-resources department worth their salt would have rejected nearly all of Jesus' men for consideration of continuing His ministry. They lacked the background, education, and vocational aptitude to propel Jesus' work into the next two thousand years.

Simon Peter, Andrew, James, and John were blue-collar fishermen. Simon Peter, the ringleader of the four, was prone to fits of rage, while James and John had a reputation for being overly outspoken. The latter two also tended to play for themselves, rather than as a team.

Thomas was a cup-half-empty naysayer (the negative and gloomy Eeyore of the bunch), constantly questioning the decisions being made for him and doubting the claims of Jesus' resurrection. His personality would slow down any decision-making process, undermining company morale. Matthew's background as a get-rich-quick-at-the-expense-of-others tax collector would raise serious questions about his integrity on any project. James the son of Alphaeus, spent time as a Jewish terrorist. His radical leanings would endanger any sensitive project.

One disciple, however, would have appealed to any human-resources department as someone with great potential, resourcefulness, a keen business mind, contacts in high places, ambition, and responsibility. Of the twelve disciples, this man was perhaps the most likely to be deemed qualified and quickly trusted to organize and manage a movement into a stable, prosperous, and growing organization.

His name? Judas Iscariot—a life of promise with a disastrous ending.

These are the men Jesus chose to lead the most important movement in history!

If you and I had been making the decisions, we likely would have rejected the Eleven as underqualified, overly flawed and, well, too ordinary. They just didn't display the talents and abilities typically associated with undertaking such important roles in perpetuating God's Kingdom plan.

And maybe that's the point.

By consistently choosing weak and imperfect men and women (who often came from lowly circumstances) like Abraham, Jacob, Rahab, Gideon, Ruth, David, Mary, Matthew, Peter, and the other disciples to do His important Kingdom work, He sent an emphatic message from heaven.

Just like choosing a stable in a small town to be the birthplace of His Son, God reinforced the message by choosing imperfect people to do His work. When He chose carpentry, not rabbinical ministry, to be Jesus' vocation, He emphasized His message again.

Later on, when He chose for His Son—the King of Kings and Lord of Lords—to ride into Jerusalem on a donkey for His "triumphal entry," He was making sure we didn't miss the point.

And finally, when God chose for Jesus to die a criminal's death on a lowly cross, rather than a hero's death, He was putting an exclamation point on the message He'd been communicating all along:

> *God does extraordinary things through ordinary (and even lowly) people and circumstances.*

He always has … and He still does.

The Problem with Spotlights and Platforms

Jesus, who started this eternal movement, gave the church an example to follow. He surrounded Himself with flawed people who had average gifts. He equipped them during His short time on earth and then empowered them by giving them His Holy Spirit. The result? They spread a world-changing message and movement in every direction.

So why does the North American church look so different from the New Testament church? Where did we lose track of the values Jesus gave us and deviate from His plan for reaching the world?

It seems that we've diluted His Plan A for reaching the world. We've distorted it. Added to it. Subtracted from it. Forgotten parts of it. Combined it with *our* plans. And as a result, it hardly resembles the plan Jesus laid out for us.

Somewhere along the way, we shifted our ministry focus from the mainstreams of life to the main stages of our sanctuaries. And in doing so, we unwittingly communicated that God does His most significant work through a small percentage of Christians endowed with platform gifts. For some time now, our ministry heroes have been primarily limited to "Christian celebrities"—talented musicians, dynamic speakers, best-selling authors, high-energy televangelists, powerful Christian leaders, and well-known pastors.

While these high-profile people *have* impacted the Kingdom of God in very significant ways, more Christian celebrities aren't the answer to the great harvest need! Of course, it's true that main-stage ministers contribute critical Kingdom work. We need church leaders, pastors, teachers, and others like them to equip God's people for Kingdom service. But has it ever bothered you that the North American church's hunger for high-impact ministry differs so greatly from Jesus' approach? Why don't we champion the ministry potential of ordinary people who do ordinary things in ordinary places? Why have we become enamored with up-front celebrity forms of ministry that occur in the spotlight and on the platform? Why have so many Christians accepted their sorely misguided destiny: to live unimportant, mundane, low-influence lives? This is not God's intention.

Everyone yearns to personally experience the love of God, tangibly expressed in and through the lives of countless faithful Kingdom laborers. Rather than call a few select people to make a difference, God's strategy is to mobilize a vast army of laborers who go into every place of need in every corner of the world. Significant Kingdom work will be accomplished by nameless, faceless people who do what they can where they are—with God adding the increase to their labor. That's God's Plan A.

This passion fueled the Protestant Reformation led by Martin Luther five centuries ago:

> [It is a] false assumption that there is a special calling, a vocation, to which superior Christians are invited to observe … while ordinary Christians fulfil only the commands.… There simply is no special religious vocation."†

Luther's term *superior Christians* referred to people who had taken a monastic vow—the clergy. In our day, the "superior Christian" probably represents the person who does ministry on a stage or in a spotlight.

I believe that God wants us to complete the Reformation work He began with Martin Luther centuries ago. He's kindling a movement of commonplace laborers and calling every one of us to join Him in His work. There's no exclusivity in His employment plan. The word *laborer,* which Jesus used to describe His plan for the world, is an all-inclusive word. It's an "everybody" word.

All of us—no matter what role we play in the Kingdom—have a meaningful, influential, and critical role to play. No exceptions. *You* matter to God and His plan.

Ask your unbelieving neighbors and friends what they think of Jesus, and many will tell you they're impressed with Him. They like most of what He said and did. But in many cases they'll quickly add that they don't have such high regard for most churches. They think churches focus more on well-orchestrated worship services than loving people in the mainstreams of life like Jesus did.

I wonder if our neighbors would have a different opinion of our churches if we primarily invested in Plan A ministry that equipped and mobilized ordinary people to love and serve others in the mainstreams of life.

It's time for us to return, recover, renew, and revitalize the fullness of God's Plan A in our generation. It's time to let it once again guide the church into the future.

Grandma Grace's Legacy

Grace passed away a few years ago. The kingdom of darkness was no doubt glad to see her go. But the impact of her life will be felt for decades to come, as her "spiritual grandsons" influence the lives of others.

Grace's life was a living sermon to all of us who knew her. It reminds us that God still wants to use all of us in unimaginable ways to reach the world. It reminds us that all we must provide is the ordinary and that He will provide the extraordinary.

Paul Billheimer once wrote, "The fate of the world is in the hands of nameless saints." Not Christian celebrities. Not up-front personalities. Not "superior" Christians.

The fate of the world lies is in the hands of commonplace laborers like Grace the Grandma and James the Roofer. It lies in the hands of people like you.

Endnote

† Martin Luther, quoted at The Quotable Christian, www.pietyhilldesign.com/gcq/quotepages/discipleship.html (accessed October 27, 2009).

Three
Being You-nique

Around the time I married Dawn, I was serving as a young pastor in a church. And, like many pastors' wives, Dawn was scrutinized by people in our new church to see if she fit their expectations of an ideal pastor's wife.

She didn't.

"Does she play the piano?" an older woman in our new congregation asked me. She didn't.

"Well, does she sing solos?" the woman continued. She didn't do that either.

"Well, *surely* she can lead a women's Bible study," the woman persisted.

"No," I answered, "that's not Dawn's gift."

"Well, *what does she do* that would make her a good pastor's wife?" the woman asked in frustration.

Truth is, Dawn has many unique and wonderful gifts and talents. But she doesn't fit the mold that some have wanted to squeeze her into.

She can't play an instrument, but you should see her flair for art and color. She doesn't sing, but she's great at welcoming people into our home—and wow, can she cook! She can't speak in front of groups, but she thrives in interpersonal settings.

That's how God has wonderfully designed my wife.

Early in our marriage, Dawn traveled with me as I spoke at different ministry events around the country. Sometimes event hosts mistakenly assumed that she was available to speak—and they would try to book her as well. Without telling us, one host scheduled her to speak for a women's group at the same weekend conference where I was speaking. By the time we found out, we felt it was too late to cancel.

In the days leading up to the event, Dawn grew increasingly terrified. She hardly slept the night before—which is rare for her—and she hardly ate anything the day of the event. As she was about to leave our hotel room for the meeting, I could see her hands trembling. I gave her the best reassuring hug I could give and prayed the most earnest prayer I could pray. After she left, I alternated between pacing our hotel room and getting on my knees to pray.

Two hours later, she returned to our room. Clearly relieved, she tossed her notebook onto the table and plopped down into a chair.

"How did it go?" I asked excitedly.

After taking a deep breath, she smiled. "Well, before this, *I* knew I couldn't speak. And now, every woman who was in that room knows it too. And I'm sure they're now telling all their friends that I can't speak. And I hope their friends tell the whole world that Dawn Robertson is not a speaker!"

We laughed about it for weeks.

God Specially Gifts Everyone for Ministry

Dawn needed a little more time to discover God's unique ministry design for her life. She realized her ministry sweet spot wasn't on a stage or behind a microphone. The same is true for many of us. We need time to discover our ministry sweet spots. Oftentimes we find them in our homes and neighborhoods.

A few years ago, shortly after moving into a new neighborhood, Dawn began building relationships with some of the women who lived on our street. Not many of them knew each other, so she invited them to our home one Saturday to get to know each other while enjoying her delicious breads and incredible desserts.

At her request, I prayed a commissioning prayer over her—like we prayed over James the Roofer. When we finished, I gathered the kids and left the house.

Before long, our home was full of neighborhood women. So many came that they filled up the kitchen, dining room, and living room—even overflowing into the backyard. They enjoyed their time together so much that they stayed and stayed, long past the designated time. They wouldn't leave!

Four hours later, Dawn asked them if their families might be looking for them. They finally trickled out the front door—smiling, laughing, and excited about their opportunity to get together. Dawn assured them it wouldn't be the last.

It wasn't. They began meeting regularly in our home. And as time went on, their conversations turned to deeper matters. Dawn started spending one-on-one time with different women outside the gatherings. And as she did, God began to move.

One woman brought her family to church for the first time. Another decided to work on putting her marriage back together. Another young woman became a follower of Jesus.

Dawn discovered that her ministry sweet spot existed in the *mainstream* rather than on the *main stage*. She simply hung out with people where they lived—where they were comfortable.

Many of our neighbors would have felt uncomfortable setting

foot in a church building. Instead, Dawn brought the church to them. She was their pastor. Our kitchen and dining room served as their sanctuary. The dining-room table (full of delicious baked goods) operated as Dawn's platform. Meaningful conversation was their music. And Dawn's life acted as a microphone, amplifying the wonder and truth of the Scriptures in front of them.

No professional minister could have reached our neighborhood like that. God uniquely positioned and gifted Dawn for building the relational bridges needed to reach into the women's hearts and lives. And she was available.

That's the kind of ministry God has designed for Dawn. That's her ministry sweet spot.

Handmade by God

God uniquely designed each of us with a ministry purpose in mind. No clones, copies, or dittos exist in the Kingdom of God. We all have been given a unique role in carrying out His Plan A. And you'll only frustrate yourself—and sometimes others—when you try to play a role that doesn't belong to you.

You are not mass-produced and lined up on a department-store shelf—each product resembling the other. Instead, you are a handcrafted, one-of-a-kind being.

Think about the difference. Mass-produced items experience identical creative processes. The goal for mass-producing is efficiency—producing the most identical items in the least amount of time.

Handcrafted items, on the other hand, are made individually. They require time and effort involving great thought and care. No two are exactly alike. That's the way God designed you and me.

Psalm 139 tells us that we're "fearfully and wonderfully" made. God personally involved Himself in the design of our bodies and our lives (Psalm 139:13–16). Sounds a lot more like handmade than mass-produced, doesn't it?

The apostle Paul explained God's careful design involving our lives this way: "For we are God's *workmanship*, created in Christ Jesus *to do good works*, which God *prepared in advance* for us to do" (Ephesians 2:10).

This passage offers rich insights into the way God created us. Paul says that God took great care in designing you. The word *workmanship* conveys the idea of a master craftsman who takes pride in the fine details of his work. The Greek word translated as *workmanship* is *poiema*, which means "that which has been created."

Does *poiema* sound familiar? We get our English word *poem* from it. The Greek word even gives the connotation of a "work of art." In fact, some versions of the Bible translate *poiema* as *masterpiece*.

You are God's masterpiece. *You* are His poem. *You* are His work of art.

When we look at ourselves this way, we begin to understand our incredible value. If Rembrandt's artistic masterpieces have great, undisputed value, wouldn't God's one-of-a-kind human masterpieces convey even greater value?

This passage also says that God designed each one of us for a reason. We were uniquely created to do specific good works that God determined for us before we were born. In other words, you and I were created *on purpose*. And He's designed us in a way that will enhance our effectiveness as we live out our ministry purpose.

Furthermore, this passage implies that there's no exclusivity in

God's Kingdom-employment plan. What good news! Jesus is an equal-opportunity employer! This means God wants to strategically employ *you* in the work of His Kingdom—using your career, hobbies, past experiences, gifts, talents, and everything else that's unique about you.

That's an important part of His Plan A.

God Doesn't Make Photocopies

In a world inhabited by more than six billion people, it would be easy to assume that there's nothing truly unique about you. But there is.

You have something that's physically different from any other person who's ever lived. It has belonged to you since you were in your mother's womb, and it will remain unchanged throughout your life. It's a small window into God's totally unique design for you. What is it?

Your fingerprints.

The arches, whorls, and loops on your fingers create a pattern unlike anyone else's. If God took that much care in designing your unique fingerprints, He must intend for you to be different in other ways, too.

Crime investigators have long used fingerprints to identify people who were present at a crime scene. And the same trail applies to the unique ministry imprint you leave on the everyday lives of the people you touch.

Paul wrote about God's purpose in designing His one body of believers out of many different parts. God gives each of us different roles and responsibilities (Romans 12; 1 Corinthians 12;

Ephesians 4). Paul declared that each part is vitally important—even the ones that are hidden or don't seem important (1 Corinthians 12:22–23). But together, each part functioning according to God's plan, they act as one. In fact, the body parts working together resemble Jesus (1 Corinthians 12:27).

Imagine the overwhelming joy you will experience as you fulfill the unique and distinct ministry role that God specifically designed for you. But, as my wife, Dawn, will quickly point out, you'll get frustrated if you try to fulfill someone else's role or try to fulfill your role in exactly the same way as someone else. God doesn't make photocopies! Your role and style were intended by God to be different.

You don't need to imitate anyone else. God has designed you like no other, and His design is perfect for the ministry He's called you to. In a sense, He's given each of us a ministry fingerprint.

Understanding our unique design occurs most naturally as a result of an intimate relationship with God and His Word. Studying God's Word and meditating on His historical tendency to choose ordinary people and ordinary things to accomplish His extraordinary purposes should give us great confidence. Take, for example:

- the slingshot David used to slay Goliath (1 Samuel 17:40)
- the jawbone Samson employed to defeat the Philistines (Judges 15)
- the staff God gave Moses to lead the Israelites out of Egypt and into the Promised Land (Exodus 4)

- the handful of flour and small portion of oil that fed Elijah and the widow of Zarephath's family for three years (1 Kings 17)

- the widow's meager offering (Mark 12)

- the boy's lunch that fed five thousand (John 6)

God often chooses "the foolish [simple, small, unexpected] things of the world to confound the wise" (1 Corinthians 1:27 KJV). When God's all-surpassing power shows up in the simplest of people and things, there's no mistaking it (2 Corinthians 4:7). The story and the glory are all His.

Ministry That Looks Like You

Discovering the good works for which you were created can be difficult. Why? If you focus solely on the church (just one of many places you can serve God and others for a few hours a week), you may have a hard time finding a ministry expression that looks like you. The choices can seem pretty limited.

For far too long, we've confined our understanding of ministry to a tight little mental box, believing it contains a very limited number of expressions. Fortunately, ministry doesn't need to be limited by a building or a weekly gathering. It can be wildly creative and entrepreneurial. God can employ nearly everything from your life for ministry to others—even some of the things that you may not readily associate with ministry.

For instance, have you ever thought about using your interests and hobbies as a basis for ministry? I have friends who turned the activities they enjoy into powerful expressions and extensions of Jesus. Here are some examples:

> Ian loves to fly-fish and teach others how to do it. He also loves to share his faith in God with others. So, he decided to combine the two. Ian invites his non-Christian friends on weekend trips into the Colorado Rocky Mountains, where he teaches them to fly-fish. The long car ride into the mountains and the long hours of fishing give Ian plenty of opportunities to discuss spiritual matters with his friends. He calls his ministry "Life on the Fly."
>
> Brittany loves to read books, so she started a book exchange with other women in her community. Before the women arrive, she places brand-new, beautiful Christian books on the tables for them to peruse and possibly read. Brittany enjoys watching how many people leave with her "special books," knowing their lives will be powerfully impacted. The book exchange also provides her a natural opportunity to build relationships with other readers and to share her spiritual beliefs during their book discussions. She's intuitively doing Plan A "by the book."
>
> Ryan loves gourmet coffee. Wanting to use that passion to minister to others, Ryan struck a deal with the owner of a struggling coffee shop in his small Midwest town that he'd bring in paying customers to the shop if he could lead Bible studies there with them. Over time,

Ryan's one-on-one meetings with friends turned into a coffeehouse-style ministry that eventually led him into hanging out with unbelieving young adults in his community. Many became followers of Jesus through Ryan's relational influence—as he connected with them around a cup of coffee.

Megan is a nurse who played volleyball in high school. When the opportunity came up recently, she joined a volleyball league with her coworkers. The experience has helped her get to know them better and has produced opportunities for her to engage in significant spiritual conversations with many of them.

Rusty is an experienced hunter. He started a regional club for people who share his love of hunting. Each year, Rusty organizes a wild-game cook-off night that includes, as a part of the evening's program, a brief testimony shared by another Christian hunter.

Scott is a thirtysomething skateboarder. Back in the day, he could perform some pretty amazing tricks on his board. He's right at home hanging out at the local skate park. Despite his work responsibilities and a growing family, he still loves all things skateboarding—just like he did when he was a kid. He still loves to read about it, talk about it, teach others how to do it, and—every once in a while—show that he still has some skills. Scott also loves to share his incredible story about how God saved him from a life of drugs and despair. He now strikes up spiritual conversations with skaters at the skate park—usually after he teaches them some new tricks!

Corrine loves kids. She began reading parenting books and joining parenting groups of different kinds when she started having children. As her four kids grew older, they began bringing their friends home—and she became a second mother to them. She started hanging out with other neighborhood moms at the park and swimming pool. And she began developing friendships with other soccer parents at her kids' practices and games. Being a mom has provided her with a great platform from which to minister to other kids and their parents.

Jason loves all kinds of sports—especially soccer. He played competitive soccer growing up, and now he volunteers as a coach for his community's youth soccer league. Throughout each season, Jason prays earnestly over his team roster like a dad would pray over his child. He knows that, for some on his team, he's the closest thing to a praying dad they'll ever have.

After seventeen years of marriage, Rick and Kathy were satisfied living without any children of their own. But through his work as judge in the juvenile court system, Rick became increasingly aware of the need for older children to

> be placed in healthy homes, and he could no longer ignore the problem. When a boy named Ben came up for adoption, Rick and Kathy knew it was time to expand their family. Soon, they also added Sara and Daniel and then Jae. Before long, they had adopted four more, bringing their total to eight children! "The Bible clearly states that true religion means taking care of children and widows," Rick explained. Leading magazines and television news stations have featured this radiant Christian family of ten. Their passion for family has become an everyday Plan A lifestyle and a beacon to others watching them.

Ian, Brittany, Ryan, Megan, Rusty, Scott, Corrine, Jason, and Rick and Kathy have all found ministry expressions that look like them—based on what they already love to do.

What do *you* love to do?

Wouldn't you love for God to show you how you can employ *your* gifts, passions, and abilities to serve Him and bless others? Get creative and entrepreneurial!

Laborership (a word I made up) doesn't have to be lifeless and boring. In fact, there's a growing movement of entrepreneurial people who are finding laborership both joyful and exhilarating because they've smashed the small box they'd previously placed around ministry. They've recognized and embraced the reality that just about every aspect of life has relational ministry potential.

So why not explore your own uniqueness and begin to experience the ministry assignment God has designed for you?

Four
Everyday, Up-Close Heroes

Where were you the morning of September 11, 2001?

Do you remember exactly where you were and what you were doing and feeling when the shocking news of the terrorist attacks on New York City and Washington, D.C., first reached you?

Do you recall the sickening feeling of horror that came over you while watching the initial television images of the two airliners crashing into the World Trade Center? The television news reports played the footage over and over until it was so deeply ingrained in our minds that we could think of little else.

Over the next two days, the news was dominated by reports on the rising death toll, families seeking missing loved ones, and speculation about who orchestrated the attacks and where they might strike next. The media didn't offer much hope to calm our fears.

Then, hopeful stories about survivors and heroes began to surface.

Passengers aboard one of the planes sacrificed their lives to bring it down before it could crash into another building and kill countless others. Volunteers across America donated blood and money, doing whatever they could to assist in the rescue and recovery efforts.

And then stories emerged about ordinary police officers and firefighters who risked their lives to save others at the scene of the World Trade Center attack.

If you're an American, you probably agree that these stories played a pivotal role in our healing and recovery. They helped us refocus our attention onto something good and hopeful. After witnessing such horrific evil, we needed these stories of heroes to remind us that humans are still capable of doing good. And the stories helped us understand the importance of ordinary laborers in our moments of desperation.

Prior to September 11, celebrities defined our perception of heroes. But at least temporarily, this tragic loss seemed to change our definition.

Many celebrities did their best to help in the days after the attacks. Actors and athletes raised money to support recovery and cleanup efforts. And politicians made sure that frontline workers were mobilized and supported. But for the most part, they did their work from a distance.

Unfortunately, only so much can be done from a distance.

In our moments of desperation, few of us look to the closest celebrity for help. We need people who can meet us where we are with what we need in that moment.

We need people who are *up close.*

The men and women trapped beneath the rubble at ground zero needed more than help from a distance. They needed immediate, sacrificial help from people right there. They needed firefighters, police officers, and all forms of emergency workers.

They needed able-bodied people on the scene.

The same holds true in the Kingdom of God. God is seeking highly committed, on-the-scene heroes who will bring His love up close to others in need.

Jesus called them laborers.

Average Christians need to see themselves as vital, daily

dispensers of God's grace. They must embrace their role of bringing God's love up close to others. We *impress* people from a distance, but we *impact* them when we're up close. Why? Because when we're up close to others—at work, at home, at school, in our neighborhoods, in our communities, and elsewhere—we bring God up close to them as well. Many of the people we come into contact with every day try to keep God at a distance. But keeping His laborers at a distance isn't so easy.

What if we spent our lunch hours developing relationships and made our homes, apartments, decks, and porches into hospitality centers?

What if we ventured out of our comfort zones and met our neighbors? And what if we began responding to their social invitations?

What if we stopped spending all of our social time with our Christian friends and began spending intentional time with unbelieving friends?

What if our highest daily prayer was to lead impacting lives, not impressive ones?

What if we noticed overlooked people and needs, traveled off the beaten paths of our lives, and moved up close to the poor and marginalized in our communities and beyond?

What if instead of pursuing spotlights and stages, we looked around for the mud puddles of human need and waded in them?

Imagine how we'd usher God's presence—up close—into the lives of others!

I spoke about this kind of ministry to a group of college students in one of the intense summer laborer-training programs hosted by Kingdom Building Ministries. At the end of the program, a young man named Zach approached me and shared his summary of what it means to be a Plan A laborer:

> Being a laborer is just hanging out with people, loving them, and sharing God with them whenever you get the chance. *Everyone* can do that!

It was simple yet profound.

Getting up close to people.

Hanging out with them.

Loving them in practical ways.

And sharing God with them.

I'm not big on formulas, but that's pretty close to what Jesus did. And Zach was right: It's a model that *anyone and everyone* can follow.

No wonder his denomination says he's one of the most successful missionaries they've ever seen—and he's still a really young guy. He's just been following the up-close ministry strategy that Jesus modeled.

Our Up-Close, On-Location Impact

God wants our 24/7, "on location" laborership because when *we* are up close to others—where we live, work, and play—*He* is up close to them as well.

And God wants to be up close to people. It's the reason He sent His only Son to earth in the form of a person like you and me. Why did Jesus—who was "in very nature God" (Philippians 2:6)—leave His throne room in heaven and come to this world? Because He loved us and wanted to be with us.

Jesus, the Word made flesh, proclaimed that the Kingdom of God was at hand. Suddenly, the Kingdom (the ways, love, rule, and reign of God) was within reach of everyday people like you and me. They touched and "beheld" the glory of God. Rather than an up-front show, Jesus gave people an up-close encounter.

Hundreds of years before Jesus' birth, God disclosed His up-close intentions through the prophet Isaiah:

> Therefore the Lord himself will give you a sign: The virgin will be with child and will give birth to a son, and will call him *Immanuel.* (Isaiah 7:14)

Matthew repeated this prophecy again in his account of Jesus' birth, but he goes one step further. He explains what "Immanuel" means.

> "The virgin will be with child and will give birth to a son, and they will call him Immanuel"—which means, "God *with us.*" (Matthew 1:23)

God *with us.*

Did you catch that? When Jesus came to earth, God was with us.

God is a relational being who desires to be in a relationship with us. He wants to know us and be known by us. Rather than a deistic God who created the world and then left us to fend for ourselves, He wants to be intimately involved in our lives—even our messes.

Eventually, Jesus ascended back to His throne in heaven. But He still didn't leave us alone. He sent His Holy Spirit to be our constant companion in this life.

God is still *with us*.

If you're still not convinced that God wants to be up close to us, just read Jesus' famous last words before leaving earth. Now, before you read them, remember that people often share what's foremost on their hearts when they know they're speaking their final words.

What were Jesus' final words before leaving earth?

> Surely I am *with you always,* to the very end of the age. (Matthew 28:20)

Jesus said He would always be with us. He desires to live out His title as Immanuel *to* every one of us. But that's not all. He also wants to be Immanuel *through* us to others as well. Many who wouldn't otherwise embrace God's presence in their lives are exposed to His love and goodness through us.

When God is with us, He goes wherever we go. According to 1 Corinthians 3:16, God makes His home in us. So when we show up on the everyday scenes of other people's lives, He's there too. As we're up close to others, God is up close to them too.

How do you become God's Plan A? Simply get up close to people, hang out with them, love them in practical ways, and share the God who lives in you with them.

Everyone can do that.

Five
Living in the Mainstream

Years ago, I spoke in the Dominican Republic for a ministry that works with American kids struggling with behavioral problems. I addressed them several times a day during their spiritual-emphasis week.

Early in the week, I met a young student who showed me what Plan A can look like lived out.

Lance approached me after one of my teaching sessions and asked if he could talk with me. Later, he shared what had been happening in his life that week. Clearly, God was lighting a fire in his heart.

Lance explained that he had entered the program not because he was rebellious or had broken the law like many of the other kids. His parents asked him to enter the program so he could gain more structure and discipline in his life.

"I've gotten a lot out of my time here," Lance said, "but now I'm thinking it may be time to go home. I want to help people learn more about God. Maybe I could make a bigger difference in the lives of my old friends. What do you think, Dwight?"

"You may be right," I replied. "But is it possible that God is giving you a temporary assignment while you're still here? Is it possible that He wants to use you to minister to kids right here while you're with them?"

Lance's eyes lit up as I continued sharing with him a vision for his temporary assignment.

"That's it!" he suddenly exclaimed. "There is something I can do for the other kids while I'm still here! I know things about their lives their parents don't know—stuff not even our staff knows. I'll pray for them and talk with them as God leads. Dwight, some of them are pretty messed up. I hope I can help."

Over the next few days, Lance and I chatted about his newfound purpose for the rest of his time in the Dominican Republic. I gave him a book on prayer, and we prayed together for some of the other kids from his dorm—including a kid named Chris, who professed to be an atheist.

After I left the campus, Lance and I continued to write back and forth. In one letter, he wrote,

> The other day, Chris announced at the dinner table that he is no longer an atheist. I have now changed my prayer from, "Lord, please show Chris that you're real" to "Lord, Chris needs to know you personally. Please help him make the decision to accept and follow you." The power of prayer is really strong!!!

Unfortunately, that was the last letter I received from Lance. A few weeks later, one of the program administrators called me on the phone.

"Are you sitting down?" she asked. "There's been an awful tragedy here this week. A group of boys from one of our dormitories was swimming in the river. A flash flood suddenly swept three of the boys downstream, including Lance. We rescued two of them, but we couldn't reach Lance in time … Dwight, I'm sorry to tell you. Lance is dead."

I sat in stunned silence, trying to figure out how to respond. The administrator paused for a moment to let the difficult news sink in, then continued.

"Dwight, there's more I want to tell you. As we were cleaning out Lance's locker and sorting through his belongings, we came across some things you sent him—encouraging letters and a book about prayer. The book had highlights and notes all through it. We also found his prayer journal. We're amazed at how many kids and situations he was praying for. We've been piecing together a lot of recent things that have been happening as a result of Lance's prayers."

She went on to share specific answers to prayer. Discouraged staff members ready to give up experienced new strength, joy, and purpose in their work. Students struggling for years with emotional and spiritual issues showed new signs of growth and victory. Even some of the most troubled kids experienced major breakthroughs in their attitudes and behaviors.

"We now realize that Lance prayed for those needs," she said. "And God answered his prayers! We're amazed. Single-handedly, a teenage kid impacted our program, staff, and students through his prayers."

Several weeks later I learned that five kids gave their lives to Christ at Lance's funeral. One of them was Chris, the former atheist. He had watched Lance's life more closely than anyone realized. He experienced God's love through Lance before he even believed God existed.

Chris and the other kids embraced God's love because a fellow student caught a vision for the role he could play in their lives—as one who was up close to them.

God wants to give *you* a vision for the role you can play in the lives of the people around you—on your assembly line, in your office, your neighborhood, your dormitory, or your class at school. Perhaps He wants you to pray for their needs—becoming their first-ever prayer intercessor. Perhaps He wants you to be His agent for meeting their needs. Perhaps God wants you to be a living testimonial of His love and grace that they *see* and *feel* firsthand.

Lance the Student followed Jesus' example of becoming God's up-close, on-the-scene connection to the kids in his sphere of influence.

And God did the rest.

Mainstream versus Main Stage

God gave Lance a *mainstream* ministry rather than a *main-stage* ministry.

Think about it. Chris and the other kids who made spiritual decisions at Lance's funeral heard me speak during that spiritual-emphasis week in the Dominican Republic. Who knows? God may have planted some seeds in their hearts through my messages.

But who made the greatest impact on those kids? It wasn't a man on the *main stage* but a boy in the *mainstream* of their lives.

They were exposed to my *words* for a few days. They were exposed to Lance's *life* (and prayers) for many months—and their lives were impacted forever.

That's not to say that main-stage ministry has no purpose or impact. It's provided me the personal privilege of sharing with thousands about God's love and truth.

But in the mainstreams of life we get to interactively share God's love and truth in up-close relationships, where our lives bear witness to God's love and power. And most people who don't know—or don't want to know—Jesus will unknowingly watch a mainstream life before they knowingly listen to a main-stage sermon.

Our Mainstream Model

It's likely that Jesus' main-stage presence was powerful, but the vast majority of His ministry occurred in the mainstream. The Gospels repeatedly show the Son of Man engaging people in the mainstreams of their lives—not often at synagogues, but in life and work locations. And He didn't teach us how to do main-stage ministry (though you'd think He did by watching today's focus on up-front ministry); He taught us how to do up-close, mainstream ministry.

Jesus worked in a mainstream vocation—as a carpenter. And He chose disciples from mainstream vocations as well. Think about it: You couldn't get more vocationally mainstream in Jesus' day than carpentry and fishing. Repeatedly, God's Word calls us to "follow" Jesus—who lived a lifestyle of love and truth among everyday people.

I serve as president of Kingdom Building Ministries, an organization that sends speakers across the nation and around the world. We believe itinerant public speaking is a historically proven means for God to light people's hearts on fire and lives on purpose. Nearly every day, we receive exciting reports from speaking venues. But that's not all we hear.

We also hear many reports about individual encounters, along-the-way spiritual conversations, and behind-the-scenes, one-on-one moments where God powerfully blesses and uses our speakers in up-close ministry relationships. Why do we hear so many reports like these? Because our speakers wholeheartedly believe that their up-close ministry is as important as their up-front ministry. They must be—and are—the same, both *offstage* and *onstage*. Jesus, their hero, modeled both.

Uncontainable Faith

One evening, when my son, Dreyson, was in grade school, I arrived home from work just in time to tuck his sister and him into bed. I pulled out a sports devotional and began to read it aloud when he stopped me.

"Dad, I need to tell you something," he said a bit reluctantly. "I got called to the principal's office today at school."

Dreyson certainly had my attention. I tried to remain calm on the outside without fully revealing my shock on the inside.

Now, being called to the principal's office was the norm for me when I was a kid. In fact, people called me "Dwight the Fright" because I got into so much trouble as a kid. But a trip to the principal's office was totally out of character for my compliant, respectful, well-mannered son.

Trying to appear as cool and composed as possible, I commented in my best psychologist voice, "Tell me about it, Son."

Dreyson then delved into the details of his conversation with his principal.

"Dad, she asked what *you* do for a living, and I told her you are a minister. Then she asked where you work, and I told her you work at Kingdom Building Ministries. And after that, she asked me what Kingdom Building Ministries is, and I told her you help people love God more and help them love other people better."

I quickly complimented my son on the great job he'd done

answering a set of rather odd, intimidating, rapid-fire questions from his school principal.

"Dreyson, those were really good answers," I encouraged him. "What did she say after that?"

"Dad, she told me, '*That's* the problem.'"

I was confused. "*What's* the problem?"

"She said that I'm not supposed to talk about God at school. I'm not supposed to talk about Him in class, in the hallways, out on the playground, or in the cafeteria. She even told me I shouldn't talk about Him in our neighborhood or at the park. She said I could only talk about Him inside our house or a church building. That's it! Nowhere else. And she's the boss of our school!"

Dreyson looked intently at my face to see my response.

"Son, are you an American?" I asked.

He gave me a confused look. "Yes, Dad, of course I am."

"Well, the last I checked, every American has two important rights that your principal is trying to overstep. Those rights are called the freedom of speech and the freedom of religion."

"What's that mean, Dad?"

I explained to Dreyson that those rights gave him the freedom to talk about Jesus at school and in other public places. He grew increasingly excited as I gave him the details.

He couldn't wait to get to school the next day to exercise his rights.

"Okay, Dreyson," I responded, "let's bring balance and courtesy to all this. Exercising this freedom also means you treat people with respect, honor, and diplomacy." In just a little while he understood the balance—as much as a young student can.

Several weeks later at dinner, Dreyson announced that he had some exciting news.

"Tommy gave his life to Jesus today in the school cafeteria!" he exclaimed. "I saw him sitting by himself at lunch, so I sat down next to him. Over lunch I talked to him about God."

He paused and looked over at me. "Dad, he had never heard anything about God. He didn't even know the meaning of Christmas. I told him about Jesus and asked him if he wanted Jesus to be in his life like He is in mine. He said yes, so I prayed with him. Dad, we have to get him a Bible soon. They don't have one at their house."

I was so excited to witness my son taking his faith into the mainstream of his everyday life. Tommy's life depended on it.

Dreyson's principal had tried to squelch his voice and limit his faith to within the four walls of a church building. But she didn't understand that Dreyson's faith and his God were much too big to be contained by any walls.

While Jesus—the Word who became flesh—attended synagogue like every faithful Jew, He modeled Plan A living again and again *outside the walls.*

You see, God is not a one-day-a-week God who waits to greet us at the front door of our church buildings. He's present everywhere. Walls cannot confine Him. And because He chooses to make His home—His temple—in our lives, we become His means to be up close to people everywhere.

As He lives *in us.* He goes where we go.

> Don't you know that you yourselves are God's temple and that God's Spirit lives *in you?* (1 Corinthians 3:16)

God's Spirit lives *in you* and seeks to be in the mainstream of life *through you.* My son understood an important truth: Buildings don't have feet; people do. No wonder God says, "How beautiful are the feet of those who bring good news" (Romans 10:15).

Our feet become beautiful as we carry God's presence outside the walls and into the mainstreams of life—bringing God's love and truth up close to people everywhere.

We're mobile churches!

As one elderly woman discovered this exciting possibility, she lamented to me, "All my life I tried to get the people who live up and down my street to come to church. I thought that was my job. And my failures over decades have been so disheartening. I didn't know there was another way. To think, all these years I could have stopped by their yards and houses, invited them over to mine, done things with them—been the church up close for them, the way Jesus modeled it for me.

"Before, I always thought I needed to bring my neighbors to a building. Now I realize *I* am that building where God makes His home. Until my neighbors enter my church building, I am going to be the outside-the-walls gal for God who wants to enter the mainstreams of their lives and be up close to them through me."

Like Dreyson did with his friend Tommy.

Beyond Buildings and Boundaries

When Jesus and New Testament writers referred to "the church," they never meant a building. The word they used referred to *a group of people called out for a specific purpose.* Buildings have boundaries that are defined by their walls—they're stationary and can't go where people can go. In fact, church buildings didn't even exist for the first three hundred years of the church.

So if we define the church as a building, we greatly limit its influence. Buildings don't have mouths, hearts, hands, or feet. People do. People can go wherever their feet take them—into neighborhoods and apartment complexes, workplaces and schools, parks and recreation centers, grocery stores and shopping malls, throughout our own communities and into foreign lands.

Think of all the places you and God visit every day. He wants to exercise His agenda of love and blessing in all those places—through you. The possibilities of bringing God's presence and purposes to people everywhere are practically unlimited!

Geographically speaking, God's Plan A for reaching the world has no boundaries.

I love looking at electronic maps with lights indicating the cities where a company's stores are located. These impressive maps reveal the company's presence and influence.

But imagine if we had a map of Jesus' Kingdom lights. Would we be astounded? Would we become more convinced than ever to believe in and multiply God's Plan A? While lighting up the location of church buildings around the world might take your breath away, imagine what a map of all God's Plan A Kingdom "life lights" would look like!

Jesus said, "*You* are the light of the world" (Matthew 5:14).

But it gets really exciting when you imagine all those life lights moving around on the map as people go about their daily lives and travels. What a powerful and meaningful visual of God's "better idea"—the body of Christ, every Plan A life light, present and moving all over the map—millions and millions of them.

Six
People to Love

My friend Camille owned a thriving travel agency in Denver. Living out God's Plan A calling on her life, she looked for opportunities to serve and share her faith with her employees and clients, and she did so effectively. As a result, her customers received far more than good travel plans.

Camille was attending a thriving inner-city church, which was a fair distance from her suburban home. Church in the City is located in the heart of Denver on East Colfax Avenue—a street known for its many homeless people, drug addicts, and prostitutes. But for the most part, this Kingdom laborer lived a safe and predictable life. Then one morning everything changed. Camille sensed God calling her beyond the four walls of her church building to a nearby street corner frequented by homeless people. Who would have thought that God wanted a red-haired, freckle-faced woman from the suburbs, who knew little about the street, to bring His love to people very different from the ones she encountered in her normal everyday world? With the blessing of her pastor, she committed to obey and began praying like crazy.

She knew that prayer is not something you do *for* the work of God—it *is* the work of God. Her first action step was praying that God would protect this plan and these people from any satanic attack that would neutralize her efforts. And she asked God to use her to bring His abundant life purpose to as many people as possible. Her praying was bold, and it needed to be! As she prayed, God poured His love into her heart (Romans 5:5).

Camille had a deep understanding that prayer is the way God prepares hearts (our own and others'). Before her first day on the street, she began earnestly praying. Eventually the time came for her to put her prayer into action. She traded her safe seat in the church sanctuary for an unfamiliar street corner. It was scary venturing outside the safe environment of a church full of "easy to love" people—to engage unpredictable new places and people. But God was leading her step by step into this unknown adventure. Answering this divine calling meant dying to self and coming alive to a life motto she would embrace again and again: *ALL for the King … for His Kingdom!*

By faith, Camille stepped out of her comfort zone, knowing those who risk nothing gain little.

Her friend Gail joined her, and together on a Tuesday morning that rocked Camille's world, they gave away free doughnuts—and a generous helping of God's love.

In her first venture into the unknown, Camille got out of her car, box of doughnuts in hand, and began walking toward a group of homeless people she'd seen earlier. Although very aware that she looked much different from them, she pushed past her fear and self-consciousness.

"Here, have a doughnut," she stammered as she offered her trembling box of doughnuts to the bystanders who suddenly stopped talking and were now staring at her.

"What's the catch, lady?" a voice offered back.

She paused and then shared what God brought to her mind.

"God loves you, and I've been praying for you. He told me to come and give you doughnuts today. I'm here to serve you. Is there anything specific I can pray for anyone about?"

For a moment, she lingered in the awkwardness of their silent stares. No one knew how to respond.

Finally, someone broke the silence. "When will you be back? Is this gonna be a regular thing?"

"Yes. Every Tuesday morning, right here at this intersection, you can have free doughnuts, friendship, a listening ear, and prayer," Camille explained.

The next Tuesday a big homeless man named Jack confided that he was headed to the hospital in a few days to have a growth surgically removed from his neck. When Camille asked to pray for him, he refused. Jack then shared that years before, a church had wounded him.

After listening intently, Camille responded, "Well, Jack, I'm your new friend. I'm not a church. And I'd like to pray for you, if that's okay. Can I?"

Street people can often discern the attitudes and motives of the people around them. Jack sensed Camille's humility and genuine concern. So in a gruff, stoic John Wayne–type voice, he replied, "I guess you can." Camille then prayed a simple prayer for Jack, the doctors, the hospital, and his recovery.

The next week, Jack was standing at the street corner, but something was missing. "Jack, where's your bandage?" Camille asked, looking for evidence of his surgery.

"When you prayed for me, the growth dissolved," he answered in a matter-of-fact voice.

Camille's jaw dropped. "It did?"

"Yeah," Jack retorted, taken aback by her surprise.

Camille was shocked.

"I really didn't have *that* much faith," Camille confessed later to me. "But God was confirming to me that if I did my part, He would surely do His."

Every time she returned, she felt God's presence and pleasure in her service to the poor. These strangers became Camille's friends and a special group of people to love.

Every Tuesday for fifteen years, Camille has served God's life-changing love to about 130 of her friends on East Colfax. And her friends love and respect her as well. She serves them breakfast, gives them hygiene items, and distributes an assortment of high-quality supplies from T-shirts to leftover Starbucks baked goods. Camille wants to bless them by acknowledging their dignity and worth. She treats them as people whom God loves and values—people with a hope, a plan, and a future.

"It's simple," Camille says. "The Holy Spirit runs it. I just keep on showing up."

But she also admits, "God had to teach me patience, faithfulness, and humility—which always usher in His presence because He opposes the proud but gives grace to the humble" (1 Peter 5:5).

God's call to take a risk and offer her efforts unto Him has required that Camille relinquish any desire for specified results or acceptable social responses.

After investing years of hugs and listening to people's stories, countless prayers, and advocating again and again on behalf of her friends, she has remained faithful. She shows up every week for the people she loves.

God has done the rest!

Now, in a donated storefront building, Camille leads a weekly Bible study for fifty street people who want to know more about

Christ, and every week God shows up in various ways. Some of her friends have plugged back into life and society. They know they can count on her—and God can too. She's a special laborer who keeps coming back, again and again. Consistency is vital when God gives you people to love.

Camille has crossed countless social, ethnic, economic, and religious boundaries in reaching out to Denver's neediest people. Today, eighty-eight lives are off the street because one ordinary woman covenanted with God to move past her own typical boundaries and find common ground with an uncommon group of people to love. Just like Jesus.

We *All* Need Jesus

Jesus loved and related to all kinds of people, regardless of their gender, age, ethnicity, socioeconomic status, education, or vocational background. He even loved the people who despised and rejected Him. And He didn't require that they be like Him in order to receive His love.

Unlike our tendency to judge people on appearance and to avoid those in need because of cultural or personal prejudices, Jesus pursued all people. He looked beyond their outer shells and sought to read and engage the inner content of their souls. He barged past typical societal cues and fence lines, ministering to all sorts of people because "the LORD does not look at the things man looks at. Man looks at the outward appearance, but the LORD looks at the heart" (1 Samuel 16:7).

Jesus modeled a spiritual conviction that none of us can ignore: Every person is *worthy of love*—no exceptions. He befriended middle-class along with wealthy folks like Joseph of Arimathea, Nicodemus, Zacchaeus, and Matthew. He unapologetically hung out with people who tarnished His earthly reputation. He touched the skin of lepers, called life into death-stinking tombs, ate dinner with hated tax collectors, and defended, conversed with, and honored women with questionable reputations. He embraced women, men, children, adults, Jews, Gentiles (even Samaritans), the healthy, unhealthy, the religious elite, thieves, prostitutes, people afflicted with evil spirits, the rich, the middle class, the poor, Roman guards, prisoners, widows, tax collectors, leaders, common laborers, sinners, and the list goes on.

C. S. Lewis wrote, "It is easier to be enthusiastic about Humanity with a capital 'H' than it is to love individual men and women, especially those who are uninteresting, exasperating, depraved, or otherwise unattractive. Loving everybody in general may be an excuse for loving nobody in particular."[†]

We forfeit God-given opportunities to change lives when we place boundaries on what we perceive as our personal capacity. All too often we give up and draw the line when we feel we've reached our capacity to love or give. In those moments when we're stretched beyond ourselves, God's internal love supply fills in our lack.

Jesus crossed boundary lines. He entered a multitude of unthinkable assignments—showcasing God's infinite love for all humanity. Then He waded into the mud puddles of human need and helped people get unstuck.

If we want to resemble the One we claim to follow, then we cannot cling to our comfort zones and cloister only with folks who look like us, talk like us, and act like us.

Living as if we have nothing in common with people who don't follow Jesus—or don't follow Jesus like we do—contradicts the core of our faith. Because God created all of us in His image, we all share in a common human experience. All of us know the joys, disappointments, and pain that life brings. And all of us long for something greater than what this world has to offer.

And we all desperately need Jesus—whether we recognize it or not.

But how can God reach those who don't recognize their need for Him if we're unwilling to wade into their mud puddles and usher His presence up close to them?

Different Is Beautiful!

In the beginning, God created the world with an infinite amount of diversity. Consider the many different animals, insects, plants, and minerals on this planet. Even after so many centuries, we're still making new discoveries about God's creation. Then add to that the billions of people who have lived over the course of time—each unique and different from one another.

God pulled out all the stops! He used the *big* box of Crayolas to create the world with endless diversity. No repetition. No duplicates. God made everyone and everything unique.

All too often, though, we fail to celebrate the blessing of diversity. Differences challenge us. So, we cluster ourselves in social (and religious) circles of sameness.

All of us feel much more at ease when we cloister around people just like us. But how much clearer would people see God's love if we boldly broke out of our clusters and crossed our uncomfortable boundary lines in order to love people *not* like us?

All of us have been more than firsthand witnesses of God's love; we've been recipients of His mercy—receiving undeserved loving-kindness and saving grace. "While we were still sinners, Christ died for us" (Romans 5:8). He loves us despite ourselves.

Could we not do likewise?

God may have placed a person in your life who isn't anything like you. In fact, you may not even like that person. But God's desire for you transcends your craving for ease or personal pleasure. He may want this man or woman to experience an undeniable truth—we are all people to love, even when we act unlovely and behave in unlovable ways. You may be the person's first-ever taste of unconditional love.

You may feel like saying, "I can't. I'm not capable. I need easier challenges."

I know how you feel.

A former boss once lied about me when I was in my late teens. He defamed my character and, I thought, ruined my future. However, God led me to His Word, requiring me not to return evil, but to love this guy and pray for him. Despite the challenge, I obeyed God. And as a result, God unleashed a new sense of freedom and effectiveness He's used to impact lives over many years. But it was an unbelievably tough love assignment.

Without hesitation, God issues love assignments that stretch us. He gave His Son a big one, didn't He?

Learning to Love

When I was a young boy, my father gently persuaded me to embrace an early opportunity for marriage preparation: learning to love my sister. He explained this would stretch me in positive ways and prepare me to be a better husband.

"But I'll get to *choose* my future spouse," I protested emphatically. "I didn't get to choose my sister. I'm just stuck with her."

He smiled, knowing she faced a greater challenge than I had—she was stuck with a brother who was difficult to love. But despite our differences, our fights grew less frequent, and we began finding the seemingly impossible ground of love that's blessed our lives to this day. We became better people in God's school of love, where learning is enhanced when people aren't the same.

Isn't that true of our *forced communities*—like work, school, and especially our families? Struggles often result from living in close proximity and being forced to work out our differences.

We're stuck dealing with generational differences between parents and children. We're stuck with gender and personality differences between husbands and wives. We're stuck with preference-oriented differences between spouses and in-laws. And we're stuck with those siblings or other family members who march to the beat of a different drummer.

And in those moments of difference, we either fold and run or we face our differences head-on and rise to new levels of personal maturity.

A Celebration in Contrast

My wife is an artist. She holds a master's degree in art and shares her knowledge and skills with her students. One art principle she has shared with me—her favorite student—directly applies to the value of being different.

An important principle in art is the beauty of *contrast*. Once, while we were walking through an art museum, she pointed to a monochromatic piece—one that used different shades of the same color. It seemed lifeless to me. Then she pointed out a piece of art next to it that combined contrasting colors, textures, and shapes. It was magnificent.

As we walked out of the museum, she pointed out that God's creation is full of the same kinds of contrast. Ever since our conversation, I've noticed and appreciated the diverse and contrasting colors, textures, and shapes in His design. It's everywhere!

We all appreciate the diversity of God's creation. Don't you enjoy going to the zoo and seeing the wide variety of animals? Don't you take pleasure in visiting an aquarium and observing the various shapes, sizes, and colors of the aquatic life? Don't you appreciate the different state and national parks that showcase the diversity of natural land and plant formations? And what about the variety of foods we eat, bursting with all kinds of different flavors?

If we see the beauty of diversity in nature, then why don't we see it in human beings?

We often gravitate toward "sameness" in our relationship choices. It's easier. But Jesus sought out all kinds of different people. He gravitated toward people unlike Himself. He ignored the "No Trespassing" signs that society constructed to keep outsiders away. And He radiated the glory of Someone who was eager to be up close with people unlike Himself.

Maybe Jesus treated people differently than we do because He viewed them differently than we do. I don't think He saw them in terms of labels—gender, race, age, social status, or other classifications—like we do.

I think He bunched them *all* into one category: *people to love.*

Since Jesus is our model, it's time we started seeing people in terms of one category too.

Real love—the *agape* love that Jesus shared unreservedly with everyone—has no categorical or relational boundaries. When we follow Jesus' model of unconditional love, we erase the categories that divide us. We embrace a life of genuine grace that melts down relational barriers and allows us to bring God up close, even to people whom others avoid or overlook. You (and your unsuspecting recipients) might be surprised by what love can do. It certainly surprised a Samaritan woman at her beverage stop one day when Jesus' atypical love broke through the typical barriers she and others were accustomed to.

Powerful things happen when we move beyond the artificial "No Trespassing" signs that people put up around themselves—or us. Sadly though, the reputation of modern-day Christians differs from Jesus' reputation in His day. While the Bible describes Jesus' reputation as a "friend of tax collectors and 'sinners'" (Matthew 11:19), today's Christians are somehow best known more for their moral objections with "sinners" than for loving them or being involved in their lives like Jesus. When was it we became so outraged by people who sin differently than we do?

I'm not saying that sin doesn't have consequences. Of course it does—in this life and the next. But we need to be careful that we avoid putting ourselves in a different category from those who don't claim to follow Jesus—or don't follow Jesus like we do.

Draw a big "people to love" grace circle. But don't forget to place yourself inside it too, because we all belong in the same category: *sinners saved by grace.* And if we're needy grace receivers, then by all means, we should be unending grace extenders.

What might happen if we loved others the same way Christ loved us—while we were yet sinners?

What might happen if we stopped seeing people as "Christians" and "non-Christians"—and started seeing them as *people to love?*

What might happen if we stopped expecting non-Christians to act like Christians, and new Christians to act like mature Christians?

What if we didn't wait until people were easier to love before we prayed for them and, instead, willingly approached them and loved them with the same love we've been blessed to receive from God?

If we did this, the "No Trespassing" signs that separate us would disappear. Defying logic by dispensing God's love, grace, and acceptance would better position us to become a foretaste of God's love and acceptance.

Our unconditional love would then serve as an appetizer for the main course of His unmatched, unbelievable, and unconditional love.

When you love someone unconditionally, you're not doing it because of something he or she has done or hasn't done. It's not an *if you* or a *when you* kind of love. Rather, it's *no matter what* love. It doesn't dispense with realities like sin, hell, or judgment, but it places abiding focus on saving grace.

Unconditional love says, "I love you, period … the way God loves me."

It doesn't condone other people's sin. It loves them in spite of it.

Love Crosses Every Line

For six years, I purposefully frequented the same restaurant, building a friendship with a server named Ahmad. As he shared with me about his life, land of origin, culture, religion, and family, I grew to genuinely love Ahmad. He became the subject of many prayers. Over time we built a friendship based on mutual respect and love that is uncommon for people of different faiths. Then, after two years of loving and listening to him, I finally shared my faith.

"I am ready for this conversation about God today because you have never treated me like a project," he told me. "You have always treated me like a person. Not many Christian people have treated me this way."

Ahmad and I shared a number of spiritual conversations after that, until he returned to his home country. I continue to pray for him and look forward to the day when we'll see each other again.

If we want to follow Jesus, then we must work to set the church back two thousand years—to a time when following Jesus meant embracing, loving, listening to, hanging out with, and serving all kinds of people—even those who look, act, and talk *very* differently than we do.

If we don't, we're creating our own Plan B just because we find it more comfortable and preferable than God's Plan A.

Endnote

† C. S. Lewis, quoted by John R. W. Stott, *The Epistles of John* in Tyndale New Testament Commentaries (Grand Rapids, MI: Eerdmans, 1964), 143.

Seven
The Domino Effect

When I was a young boy, I enjoyed spending time with my Grandma Robertson. She loved me despite my boatload of energy and hyperactive tendencies. Every time I visited her, she would greet me at the front door with a big hug, tell me fresh-baked cookies were waiting for me in the cookie jar, and then wisely focus my energy on some preplanned activity to keep me occupied and out of trouble during my stay.

My all-time favorite activity at Grandma's house was playing with her dominoes. I spent hours lining them up in masterful rows and creative formations until they blanketed her table. Meticulously setting each domino behind the previous one without setting off a premature chain reaction required concentration, which completely occupied my hands, mind, and energy for a good part of the day.

While I was hard at work—and uncharacteristically calm and focused—Grandma usually disappeared to her kitchen or retreated to the living room with a good book, occasionally talking with me from the other room. When all the dominoes were perfectly lined up, I called Grandma into the room.

Just prior to tipping the first domino over to set off the chain reaction, my grandma directed my attention to the object lesson in front of me. Maximizing the power of that moment, she instilled in me a profound Kingdom truth that has stuck with me ever since.

"Dwight, what happens when you tip the first domino?" she asked me.

"It falls, and then it makes the next domino fall, and then the next one—until all of the dominoes have fallen down."

"That's right," she replied. "Just one domino changes everything for all those others."

And then she likened my life to those dominoes. "As you reach out to tip over that first domino, think about your life—how your words and actions can have a powerful effect on others. Every time you say something to people that encourages or discourages them, you make an impact on their lives. And every time you do something that either serves or disserves them, you make an impact as well. You impact people for good or bad. And then those people go on to impact other people around them in similar ways."

But my grandma wasn't finished. She added one final touch to her object lesson.

"Dwight," she continued with a thoughtful twinkle in her eye, "if you were very, very small—so small that you couldn't see around the first domino—and if you were trying to push it over, would you know how many dominoes were going to fall?"

"No, Grandma. How could I?"

"That's right, and the same is true in your life," she explained. "When you say or do things that help others, you have no idea who you'll affect or how many people your actions might eventually affect through *them* because of the *domino effect*."

That was her signal that it was time to knock over the dominoes. Together we'd begin our famous countdown from ten and then …

"… Three … two … one … go!"

I tipped the first domino and watched the rest of them fall, one at a time—each one impacted because I intentionally touched just *one.*

The power of that lesson still resonates deep within me. All my life I've passionately believed that God calls every follower of Jesus to give a "Kingdom tip" to the domino in front of him or her. Our words and actions cause a consequential—and exponential—impact on the lives of others around us.

I once read that the most inhibited person will influence at least ten thousand people in the course of his or her lifetime. Most of us will influence far more people than that. Because of the domino effect, even the shiest person has the capacity to change the lives of countless numbers of people.

Though we seldom see past the domino in front of us, we can trust God to take our seemingly inconsequential actions of obedience—spiritually prompted prayers, inspired words, and individual encounters—to make a much wider impact over time than we could ever imagine.

Following Your Leader

Admit it. You feel your small acts of service are futile in light of the many needs around the world. How can you affect the global AIDS epidemic, poverty, or even world evangelization? But consider this: If your small acts are futile, then so were the acts of Jesus.

Jesus explained why such the vast need in the world existed when he said, "The harvest is plentiful but the [laborers] are few" (Matthew 9:37). Yet, for the most part, Jesus didn't try to reach the masses all at once. He always focused on the person directly in front of Him, performing single acts of service—and changing one life at a time. He trusted in the domino effect.

Think about it. Jesus influenced the whole world through twelve guys who were *right in front of Him*. Doesn't make sense, does it? And as He traveled from place to place, He repeatedly reached out to and focused on the *individual* directly in front of Him. Doesn't seem like the most efficient way to reach the whole world, does it? Yet His approach proved to be powerful and effective, and eventually *many* were significantly impacted.

As His follower, you can do the same. Just love the person in front of you, as God leads. You really don't have to make it any more complicated than that.

Don't waste energy worrying about the third, eighth, or eleventh domino down the line. All you need to focus on is tipping whatever one domino God has placed in front of you.

So, let's be honest. Why don't we more frequently and fully love *the one in front of us?* Perhaps we should ask ourselves these questions:

- Do I doubt God's capacity to set a powerful domino effect in motion from my smallest efforts?

- Am I hungering for a more prestigious or dramatic approach than my average everyday life seems to provide?

- Do I forget the model that Jesus repeatedly exemplified of focusing on the one person in front of me?

- Do I lose momentum deliberating about what to do next instead of trusting God to show me how to focus on the individual in front of me?

- Am I waiting for the perfect formula to tell me what to say or do—before I act?

You don't have to wait until all your dominoes are lined up and all your questions are answered before touching the person in front of you. You don't even need to have the perfect approach all figured out. Every heart has multiple entry points. Just look at the different ways Jesus responded to people's needs.

Jesus didn't live by a formula for in-the-moment acts of love. He saw the need, engaged people's hearts, and compassionately reached toward each person and situation differently.

Let Love Lead the Way

About the time Dara turned four, I began noticing some dads I greatly respected talking about their daddy-daughter date nights. I liked the idea—a lot. But quite honestly, I was … well … intimidated. I loved my daughter immensely, but I just couldn't imagine what we'd do or talk about to fill up several hours by ourselves.

Dawn began nudging me to set a date night—when Dara would be my sole focus. Of course, this also meant my dear wife would get a break, so all sides would benefit. Despite the great idea, I stalled. Then one night Dawn probed me about it.

I explained to her, "It's not that I don't want to take Dara on a date night, but what will we do? Where will we go? What will we talk about?"

Dawn offered me wisdom that at first blush didn't come across as comforting or helpful. But it made all the difference in my date with little Dara, and it launched a life of love-initiated actions ever since. She advised, "Engage your heart, Dwight. Just look into Dara's little face and get lost in her presence. Love will tell you what to do."

It didn't comfort me—at first. As much as I dislike formulas, my insecurities were so great that I wanted some kind of magic formula to materialize. But Dawn's advice didn't offer me anything easy or predictable. Besides, how would I know when love was telling me what to do?

The historic night of our date arrived. I fastened my daughter's seat belt and climbed into our Jeep. As we drove away, I asked God to give me favor with my daughter—as if I were about to enter the presence of a powerful world leader. I was ridiculously nervous.

For the first few miles, we drove in awkward silence. But then, it happened. A sweet little voice arose from inside our car. Dara was singing. Extemporaneously. Although I didn't know the words, I joined in. I sang about all her favorite things and what we were seeing as we looked out the window along the way. I sang about our "date"—and that she was my "girlfriend." Before long, we both began singing what eventually became our "date song," born that first unpredictable night.

Her face lit up as I entered her world, and I got lost in her presence—just as Dawn prescribed.

We drove to the mall and visited the shops, looking for something that would attract her interest. Our first stop was a pet store, where Dara wanted to pet a puppy. The store attendant took the puppy out of its cage and let us play with it on the floor. We were there for nearly an hour.

From time to time, I looked into her face and saw her

overwhelming joy with our simple pleasure. And once again, I got lost in her presence.

Next, we found a toy store—and she wanted to go in. As we walked around, we stopped occasionally to play with some of her favorite toys that were on display. And as we walked out of the store thirty minutes later, I once again caught a glimpse of her face. Her joy was full.

That night she sang songs. She played with a puppy and then her favorite toys. And most important, she enjoyed the full attention of her dad. That night I felt amazed, thankful, and sad that I had almost allowed my fear to rob her and me of this joyful moment.

And one last time that evening, I got lost in her sweet little face.

I learned that night how easy it is to allow fear and self-consciousness to rob us of blessing others and being blessed ourselves.

We must get over ourselves.

All we have to do is love the person in front of us. Yes, there will be times when we do something awkward and maybe even stupid. But it won't be nearly as stupid as not doing anything at all. And, yes, there will be awkward moments of silence, while we search for the right thing to say. But it won't be nearly as bad as the silence of not saying anything at all.

Loving the one *in front of you* can be scary, but it's what you were made to do. Just engage your heart, and look into that person's face. Then get lost there.

Love will tell you what to do. And the domino effect of allowing God to love through you will change not just one life, but infinitely many.

Eight
God-Issued Camouflage

"So what do you do for a living?"

Every time someone asks me that question, I usually try to conceal the specifics of my profession ... at least at first. Why? Because my role in vocational ministry usually hinders any opportunity for a normal exchange or relationship.

When they discover my profession, they often respond like a spooked deer that senses its safety has been compromised by someone who's suddenly ventured too close for comfort. As a defensive measure, they run away—either literally or figuratively.

Others who share my occupational calling understand my frustration. Our attempts to connect with people are often discounted—as if we're doing it because we're paid to, not because we want to. They act as if we're parroting some rehearsed line that all pastors are supposed to say instead of authentically caring for them or sharing from our hearts.

That's why my response to the question is usually (and truthfully), "I'm an executive with a nonprofit organization." If they ask for more information, I offer it—but if they don't, we usually delve into other conversational life topics.

At times, my title in vocational ministry has enhanced my capacity to minister to others; and, at other times, it has ... well, hindered it.

That's partly why I enjoy wearing my jeans and T-shirt—and working in my front yard or walking with my kids through the neighborhood. It's a chance to shed my ministerial title and become Dwight the Neighbor. This also provides the chance to build regular, real-world relationships as an ordinary guy.

To be honest, I prefer being a regular guy and believe that's what Jesus may have enjoyed as people saw Him through the vocational lens of a carpenter.

Over the years, I've experienced this dynamic many times.

The Perils of Being a Preacher

One summer evening a few years ago, our next-door neighbors, Chad and Julie, joined us for a cookout. Dawn and I were building a friendship with them and had even invited them to come to church with us. Although they didn't accept our invitation, we enjoyed doing other things together.

Our growing relationship was natural, fun, and relaxed … until one evening.

As we sat in our backyard, waiting for the burgers to cook on the grill, Chad began telling us about a coworker he was having a conflict with. The more he explained the situation, the angrier and more animated he became. Finally, he spewed a string of expletives that gave full expression to his anger.

"Chad, don't talk like that around Dwight!" Julie scolded her husband as she nearly jumped out of her lawn chair.

Chad gave her a strange look. "Why? Did I say something wrong?"

Then she looked at me as if we shared the same information base.

"*You* know," she stated firmly.

Her comment confused me. Chad and I had been doing things

together for a long time. I liked him a lot and had heard much worse language come out of his mouth.

Quite honestly, his heart concerned me more than his mouth. I hoped that someday a change in his heart would change the way he talked. I guess I've never believed people can be fixed from the outside in.

"I'm sorry … what's wrong?" I asked Julie. Chad and I were equally confused about her sudden offense with his everyday vocabulary.

"You *know*!" she said more firmly. But I didn't.

"Your daughter told me you're a … you know … you're a-a preacher," she said in a hushed tone—as if she were saying something bad or offensive.

"It's okay … I mean … you're so different than what I think a preacher would be like. It's okay. We've never asked a lot about each other's work and didn't know exactly what you do with the group you work with. It's funny we've never even asked each other what colleges we all attended. I guess we just started doing life together and have always talked more about current issues, hobbies, and raising our kids."

Then she quickly looked back at Chad. "So don't swear anymore around Dwight. He's a preacher!" She thought she was doing the right thing as she inflicted this death sentence on our relationship.

I did my best to keep a positive face. I acted as if it were no big deal. But my heart sank. I grieved over their sudden discomfort with me—not with me, really, but with their image and fear of "preachers." Chad and Julie's past negative experiences and perceptions of organized religion and preachers caused their comfort with me to suddenly disappear.

They no longer saw me as Dwight the Neighbor. They saw me as, you know … a-a *preacher*.

Our love for each other and the great times we'd shared in the past were now trumped by a negative perception that had brought our relationship to an impasse. I just wanted them to see me as the same regular guy they knew in the past. Before they discovered my profession, they genuinely enjoyed spending time with my family and me. We loved them, and we believe they loved us. To our disappointment, these dear friends couldn't see through their bias to the real me.

The next morning, Chad and I met each other as we pulled our trash cans to the street.

"Hey, Chad!" I greeted him. "We sure had a great time with you last night."

"Yeah, uh, thanks for having us over," he answered politely. He was clearly uncomfortable. Then he quickly darted into his house. Chad has avoided me ever since.

For several years I've worked hard to salvage our friendship and prove to Chad and Julie that I *really* care for them—that they're not one of my professional clergy projects. I feel no judgment toward them, only love. My desire has long been to live in such a way that people know my love for them transcends my career.

Ministry Camo

Looking back on that unfortunate incident in our backyard, I realize that, as a professional minister, I'm missing something that ordinary ministers like James the Roofer and Lance the Student have.

I'm missing my special ministry camouflage.

Soldiers, hunters, even nature photographers wear camo to help blend in with their surroundings. It makes them somewhat "invisible" to those who might be scared away by their presence, and it enables them to slip further into their mission territory.

In the same way, God has outfitted each of His frontline, nonprofessional ministers with camouflage. It's part of His strategy in equipping them to carry out His Plan A. For some, camouflage looks like an ordinary job—in mainstream spheres like education, health care, business, and construction. For others, it takes the appearance of a student in a school or on a college campus. And for still others, it looks like a neighbor or fellow club member.

Regardless of its appearance, camo allows you to naturally connect with people in *their* world, ministering to them out of the overflow of who you are—in the places where their pain and needs most naturally surface.

The purpose of your ministry camo is not to hide your faith or do anything covert. Rather, it allows people who have been turned off by some aspect of Christianity or organized religion to get to know you apart from their baggage. You're like an appetizer that stirs their hunger for real food—the Bread of Life. And you just so happen to know the way to the table of our Lord.

As you draw up close to Jesus while you remain up close to them, they'll smell the aroma of Christ in you and will likely want more.

To my dismay, I lose this ministry uniform when people discover I work for a ministry organization. But I gain it when people see me as Dwight the Neighbor.

Camo comes in many forms and styles, and—if you're a follower of Christ—you've been issued one, tailored just for you. What does yours look like?

Ask yourself: In what areas of my life do I naturally build relationships with people who might not rub shoulders with followers of Christ? That's your ministry uniform. It's your camo.

Take notice of it. And let God regularly employ it to bring others closer to Him.

Joe and Mary's Son

Think about it. The Father sent Jesus to earth in camouflage. He didn't enter this world with the glory that our almighty God deserves. Rather, He made Himself nothing and clothed Himself with human flesh (Philippians 2:5–8).

Furthermore, He was born into the family of a common tradesman—a construction worker (James the Roofer should feel good about that!). For many years, people knew Him only as Joseph and Mary's son—not the Son of God.

My young son loves playing army in our neighborhood with his friends. One day I couldn't find him and wanted to say good-bye before heading to the airport for an out-of-state speaking assignment. After looking for him and shouting his name into the neighborhood, I saw his head suddenly poke up from behind a bush not more than fifteen feet away—smiling triumphantly from ear to ear. His camouflage had worked!

He was delighted to be hiding so close without being detected. Perhaps the Son of God, the Savior of the world, felt just as excited about being so up close to His beloved creations without scaring them off like frightened animals.

What enabled Jesus—the Son of God and Word made flesh—to draw so near to people who previously couldn't even stand in God's presence and were forbidden from saying His name?

What made Jesus so accessible?

His humble birth in a stable to a regular dad and mom?

His beginnings in backwater Nazareth?

His exposure in His earlier years to "regular" folks and normal life, which possibly served as the subject of His easily understood parables and stories?

His experience as a construction worker?

For a while He moved around undetected and spent His time up close with all kinds of people, many of whom would have avoided getting close to the religious leaders of their day. Like my neighbors with me, they loved Jesus but didn't *really* know Him. Perhaps the full disclosure of His identity would have spooked people away. He waited awhile before asking even His closest friends, "Who do you say I am?"

The people who encountered Jesus in His everyday life didn't know they were up close to God in the flesh. His normal appearance, His parents, His humble beginnings in Nazareth, and His blue-collar vocation all played a part in His camouflage.

People felt comfortable being with Jesus. They invited Him into their homes. They asked Him to join them at their dinner tables. They shared with Him their darkest secrets. They introduced Him to their friends—perhaps they even introduced Him as "Jesus the Carpenter."

Would people have felt as comfortable with Jesus had they known him as Jesus the Rabbi or Jesus the Religious Leader? I doubt it.

Perhaps Jesus was modeling for all of us how we can share His love, grace, and truth in the camouflage of vocation and circumstance.

Even as He hung on the cross, Jesus wore the camouflage of a lowly criminal, which allowed Him to get up close to two actual lowly criminals, one of whom chose to believe in Him and join Him in heaven.

Perhaps you find yourself in a difficult situation. Maybe you struggle with a chronic health problem or a difficult work environment. Or maybe someone has betrayed you or your marriage is falling apart.

God can use your challenging circumstances to serve as camouflage so He can better position you to minister to someone else in need—perhaps in similar circumstances.

Your camouflage ministry uniform is one of the most valuable assets you have as you serve others and bring God up close to them. Do you know what yours is? Are you using it?

Nine
Meal-Table Ministry

Early in our marriage, Dawn and I developed a close friendship with Rob and Denise, an unmarried couple who'd been living together for several years.

They were very aware of our faith in Jesus, and we shared freely about it with them. When the time felt right, we invited them to go to church with us and then join us for lunch at our house afterward.

They said they'd love to, but they first needed to check their schedules before getting back with us. Two weeks passed, and they still hadn't replied to our invitation.

Finally, Denise called us late the night before our scheduled morning at church. She was very apologetic. "Dwight, I'm sorry it's taken us so long to get back with you about going to church. We don't usually respond this slowly when someone asks us to do something. But I need to be honest with you about why we've been struggling with the decision."

She explained that Rob had suffered an extremely painful church experience as a teenager and vowed that he'd never return. "I'm sorry, Dwight. We just can't go with you. But …" She hesitated for a moment and then continued. "We were wondering, could we still come over for lunch—*after* you get home from church?"

"Of course!" I replied as I assured her that I understood their struggle and how deeply sorry I was about Rob's negative church experience. "We sure do love you guys," I said as we ended our conversation.

"Who was that on the phone at this hour?" Dawn asked as I came to bed.

"It was Denise. She finally responded to our invitation."

"Really? Are they coming with us to church?"

I thought about her question for a moment. "Yes, they are," I replied. "But they're not coming to the morning service."

Dawn gave me a puzzled look. "I don't understand."

"Well, they're coming to our house for lunch *after* the service," I said. "And if you believe that the church is God's people, then, yes, they're coming to church. *We're it!*"

The next day, when Rob and Denise joined us for lunch, we delved more into Rob's past church experience. Dawn and I grieved with them as they relived the experience with us.

That day, we became the church to Rob and Denise.

Our lives became their sermon. And our meal table became their sanctuary.

They've "come back to church" at our meal table numerous times in the years since. Around our table, we've often discussed God, the church, family, work, love, and life purpose.

Jesus Modeled Meal-Table Ministry

Jesus loved spending time with people around meal tables. They were one of His favorite ministry venues. The Gospels record that He ate with, drank with, or fed people many times as a part of His ministry to them. I think it was a very intentional part of His ministry strategy.

Here are just a few examples:

- Jesus saw, stopped, and spent up-close time with Matthew and his friends at a meal table. His dining companions were not "church folk." In fact, this dinner gathering (frowned upon by outspoken religious elite) was a portrayal of "the sick" at the table ingesting the healing power of Jesus' love, grace, and what He defined as "calling"—happening at a common meal table of "sinners" (Matthew 9:9–13).

- After spotting Zacchaeus from a distance, Jesus sought the impact of an up-close encounter with this man. He went to his home and spent up-close time with him, becoming for him and his "sinner" friends the Bread of Life (Luke 19:1–10; John 6:35).

- As Jesus reclined at the meal table in the home of Simon the Leper, a "woman who had lived a sinful life" anointed Him with an expensive perfume. Jesus affirmed her actions to those sitting at the table with Him and held her up as a model for us to follow (Matthew 26:6–13; Luke 7:36–50).

- At a wedding feast, Jesus performed His first miracle by turning water into wine (John 2:1–11).

- Jesus fed fish and loaves of bread to thousands (Mark 6:30–44).

- While sharing His last supper with His disciples, Jesus showed them the "full extent of his love" by washing their feet (John 13:1–17).

- After Peter denied Jesus three times, Jesus reinstated him over a breakfast of fresh fish and bread, near a lakeshore fire (John 21:1–19).

- Sharing meal-table time together was such a well-known ministry-style of Jesus that even after seven miles of walking and talking together, it wasn't until Jesus sat down at a table and broke bread with them, did two of His disciples recognize Him after His resurrection (Luke 24:13–35).

As you can see, Jesus ministered to plenty of people around meal tables. It provided the perfect environment for the kind of highly relational, up-close-style of ministry that characterized His life.

Meal tables played such a significant role in Jesus' relational ministry that He once described Himself in terms of food and drink. He said, "The Son of Man came eating and drinking." The Pharisees also described Him in terms of food and drink. They described Jesus as a glutton and a drunkard who hung out with tax collectors and sinners (Matthew 11:19).

Although the Pharisees obviously intended to use this description as a criticism, Jesus embraced it as a compliment. It bothered the Pharisees that Jesus spent so much time eating and drinking with people. They thought His time was better spent teaching in the synagogues than hanging out at meal tables and eating with sinners (Matthew 9:11).

But the meal table was one of Jesus' favorite ministry spots. And you know what? It still is—even though He's no longer here on earth. Let me explain.

In the book of Revelation, Jesus spoke these words to the church in Laodicea: "Here I am! I stand at the door and knock. If anyone hears my voice and opens the door, I will come in and *eat with him,* and he with me" (Revelation 3:20).

Although in this passage "eating" is a metaphor that connects a physical act to a spiritual truth, we can still learn from it. This metaphor shows us that Jesus connects *eating* with *relationship.*

When we "open the door," we enter into a relationship with Jesus. In a sense, we're welcoming Him into our lives. In response, He comes in, rather than standing at the door and politely greeting us. He wants to hang out up close at the dinner table with us!

If that sounds strange, it shouldn't. Jesus did the same thing with Matthew and Zacchaeus after they let Him in. He joined them in their homes for dinner and asked them to invite their friends. Jesus "eats with us" in order to deepen His relationship with us. In a spiritual sense, He does with us what He did with His disciples so many times around a meal table. He relaxes, laughs, enjoys, converses, and lingers with us in deep relationship.

That's the power of eating together—whether we're spiritually dining with Jesus or physically gathering around a table with friends.

Lingering

Eating together plays such a powerful role because the meal table is the forum where ideas and values are naturally exchanged. No wonder it's been said that some of the world's greatest ideas were written first on table napkins. Where else would people pull up close to each other and linger long enough to share their thoughts and feelings at a deep level?

Love *expresses itself in natural ways* at meal tables.

Love *shares more deeply* at meal tables than at almost any other time of the day.

Love *lingers* at a meal tables.

Unfortunately, many families fail to eat dinner together—and lose the advantage of relational bonding that occurs in those special mealtime moments.

But it's also the reason why many families *do* guard their mealtimes. Some make sure the whole family eats around the table the majority of dinner meals each week. They fiercely guard it as an opportunity to catch up on what's happening in everyone's lives. And they won't allow TV or other technologies to distract from it.

In addition to being a connection place, the meal table is also the setting where family traditions and stories are passed from one generation to the next. Ask people where their family stories were shared, and they'll point to those relaxed mealtimes—often during holidays—when no one was in a hurry to leave the table.

They'll speak with fond memories about the hours they spent laughing and talking. When their time together was over, they left with full stomachs and even fuller hearts.

I'm probably not telling you anything you don't already know. You've likely experienced the relational power of these moments as well.

But have you ever considered it a place of ministry?

You can use meal tables to effectively minister to others in natural, highly relational, and up-close ways. Just like Jesus did with Matthew and Zacchaeus. And just like Dawn and I did with Rob and Denise.

TV Trays and Tuna Fish Sandwiches

Back in my bachelor days, I lived in a small house in a friendly, blue-collar, Midwestern neighborhood.

One of my favorite neighbors was Thelma—a kind, white-haired widow who struck me as out of place in my neighborhood. She was one of the classiest ladies I knew.

I enjoyed our fleeting moments of conversation as we ran into each other coming and going. I wanted to get to know her better. So, one day, I invited her over for lunch.

Now, there's something you should know about me: I'm horrible at making meals. As I prepared for Thelma's visit, I studied my almost-bare cupboards and realized that it was either tuna fish or peanut butter and jelly sandwiches. I chose tuna fish. I couldn't imagine making PB&Js for such a classy lady!

I cut the sandwiches into diagonal halves to add a little more class to my meal presentation and served them with some chips and tea. I settled for dining on TV trays, since I had nothing else that would function as a meal table. I whispered a final prayer as the doorbell rang, and soon, Thelma was sitting behind a TV tray. I explained that I'd just returned from a third-world country where food was scarce and asked if it was okay if I prayed to thank God for our lunch.

She politely obliged and followed my lead by bowing her head.

When I finished praying, I said "Amen" and looked up at Thelma. Her head was still bowed. I thought maybe she didn't hear me, so I said "Amen" again. She still kept her head down. *Oh no,* I thought, *she's either taking a closer look my inept culinary skills or she fell asleep during my short prayer.* Then I heard a sniffle.

That's when I realized she was crying.

"Thelma, are you okay?" I stammered.

She didn't answer right away, which set off a bit of panic inside me.

"Dwight, I'm scared," she said, continuing to look at the floor.

I slipped off my chair and knelt beside her.

"What are you afraid of?"

Thelma finally looked back at me. "A lot of my friends have died recently … and I can't sleep at night because I'm so afraid to die. It's consuming my thoughts day and night."

"What scares you most about dying?"

She paused as she pondered the question. "Dwight, I don't know what's going to happen *after* I die, and I'm afraid I'll be all alone."

Suddenly the casual environment of our TV-tray meal table became a safe sanctuary for further and deeper sharing than we'd ever experienced before.

Deep inside, I realized I was Thelma's neighbor for such an hour as this. As I shared and prayed with her, she became more than my neighbor, she became a fellow child of God. She found comfort in knowing that Jesus promised He would never leave her and that we would again be neighbors in heaven someday.

God used our meal to deliver her from paralyzing fear.

Thelma and I (along with my wife after we were married) became very good friends. Our kids called her Grandma. More important, Thelma loved and served God until she walked into the safe arms of Jesus in heaven.

What was the turning point of Thelma's life? A mealtime conversation over tuna fish sandwiches.

Our family continues to invite our neighbors into our home for meals. Sometimes, we invite one neighbor family. Other times, we invite several at once.

Occasionally, we organize block parties and invite every family in our neighborhood. Block parties offer an incredible opportunity to connect with people we hardly know—in a way that opens the door for further involvement in their lives.

Every time we invite people over for a meal, it affirms to me why Jesus did so much of His ministry around meal tables.

Another Love Language

A number of years ago, Gary Chapman wrote a book titled *The Five Love Languages*. In it, he examined several different ways people prefer to give and receive love. He lists the five "love languages" as serving, giving gifts, spending quality time with others, sharing words, and touching.

I really like his book, but I've jokingly told friends that Chapman may have missed one. I think I've found one more love language common to almost everyone: eating.

It may even be the *universal* love language!

I know it's one of mine. When I share a meal with someone, I connect at deeper levels than at almost any other time. Maybe the same is true for you. It may look different for you than it does for others. For some, the "meal table" might take the appearance of an outdoor cookout or lunch in a restaurant. For others, it may look like a corner table at Starbucks or Barnes & Noble.

Most important, meal-table ministry is something *anyone* can do. When I speak for various audiences, I often ask them, "How many of you like to eat?" They laugh a little, and nearly everyone raises a hand. "Well then," I continue, "most of you have *great* ministry potential!" We laugh about it, but they clearly get the point. Sharing a meal carries tremendous power.

Is God speaking to you about reaching people in your sphere of influence? Maybe you could meet them for coffee or invite them into your home for a meal.

It doesn't have to be formal or fancy, and it doesn't require a great deal of preparation.

Even TV trays and a couple of tuna fish sandwiches will do.

Ten

Your Story, God's Story

Your life story is composed of hundreds, perhaps thousands, of stories that offer irrefutable evidence of God's love. Your story—even just a chapter of it—might be the greatest tool in your ministry toolbox. It's not information. It's not a sermon. It's not just *a* story; it's *your* story. And everybody, cross-generationally, loves to hear stories.

Your story is more interesting to the people around you than any fact or historical figure. It's about *you*—someone they know, someone with whom they feel safe and comfortable. And they feel honored when you vulnerably share a part of yourself with them.

Real-life stories inspire belief. Like before-and-after TV commercials, your story can verify that God's loving and gracious intervention is powerful and life altering.

And you know what's great about telling your story? You're an expert on the subject! No line-by-line memorization required. You don't need a degree in theology to share what God has done in your life. Your story validates His love for you—and them.

Our stories confirm that God shows up in all kinds of situations, for all sorts of needs, in countless ways, for ordinary people like us. Imagine the hope and encouragement that provides.

Our Hurts Can Heal Others

Dawn had just arrived home from the hospital following her third miscarriage when our neighbor Diana showed up at our door. As she handed Dawn a casserole, Diana began expressing how sorry she was for our loss and then started to cry. But soon, her cries erupted into convulsive sobs right there on our front porch. Dawn quickly reached out with a hug and invited her in.

As they sat down on our living-room couch, Dawn perceived Diana's emotional response must be connected to something deeper than our miscarriage. Through her tears, Diana shared that Dawn's loss had uncovered the pain of an earlier loss in her own life—one she'd never really dealt with.

Like lava bubbling up deep within her, the years of pain—unknown to anyone—finally found their way to the surface. And through Dawn's unfolding chapter of pain and loss, God began extending His love, comfort, and healing to Diana.

Dawn became God's intimate Plan A for Diana in that moment.

In the midst of her very present pain, Dawn shared the comfort God had given her. Through their exchange of feelings, thoughts, and tears, Dawn offered a source of hope that transcended earthly friendships or anything else Diana had found.

As I reengaged Dawn just after Diana left, I told her, "Honey, no one else could've ministered to Diana like you did tonight. She needed *you.* She needed the comfort of *your* relationship with God. And she needed the hope of *your* story."

The heart-forward exchange between these two women with similar stories became God's healing balm and an opportunity for further relationship. And it also opened the door for new conversations about God.

Quick to Listen, Slow to Speak

Conversation requires listening, not just talking. And active listening earns trust. Why? Because every person wants to be heard and known. When people sense you really *want* to know them, they realize how much you value them. They appreciate that you are less self-consumed than most people—listening more and talking less.

Giving people an informational download before they feel valued or heard is presumptive and insensitive. True conversation opens doors to the kind of information sharing and enjoyable story exchange that leads to stronger and deeper relationships.

Engaging people's lives with a listening ear and asking sincere questions that probe their hearts often opens a window to their souls. Hearing them share their stories of hurt, pain, joy, and difficulty enables you to adapt what you share of God's hope, love, truth, and encouragement to their unique lives. And shouldn't it be natural for us to want to know more about other people God fearfully and wonderfully made in His own image?

Try prayerfully listening to the person, asking God where He is already at work in his or her life, how you could join Him, and what are the most important questions to ask. Listen to God, and be ready for Him to impress upon you how He wants you to love and what He may want you to say as His on-the-scene co-laborer.

Parents love it whenever other trustworthy people slow down, listen, and take an interest in their children. And you can put that same smile on God's face—and bless His creation—as you exchange stories with others.

Over time you'll become like a master tailor, sizing up the unique dimensions of someone else's life and tailor fitting your similar life stories and the gospel of God's love and truth in ways that are best suited for him or her. And it all begins with an engaged, listening ear.

God on Display

While I was catching up on some work at the kitchen table one Saturday morning, Dreyson's ten-year-old friend Cameron politely interrupted me: "Mr. Robertson, can I ask you something?"

I sat my pen on the table and looked up at him.

"Yes, Cameron, what would you like to talk about?"

"Well, Mr. Robertson, it's about your son. Could you please ask Dreyson to stop talking about God?"

"Why would you want me to do that, Cameron?"

"Because he talks about God a lot, and I don't believe in God."

"Well, Cameron, I can hardly imagine how he's going to do it," I replied. "Maybe I can ask him to stop talking about anything he's passionate about. But that means he won't be able to talk about Star Wars and World War II history, either. Okay, I'll tell him he can't talk about anything he's passionate about as soon as I'm finished here."

I tried to keep a straight face as I picked up my pen and looked back at the papers lying in front of me—as if I were going to resume my work.

"Mr. Robertson, there's no way that will work!" Cameron quickly interrupted. "I don't want you to tell him to stop talking about *those* other things! He could *never* do that."

"Hmm. You're right. It may be almost impossible for Dreyson to stop talking about Star Wars and World War II. But, you know what, Cameron? It would be even *more* impossible for him to stop talking about God. God is *much more* important to Dreyson than those other things."

Cameron walked away shaking his head. He didn't have an immediate comeback—not with me, at least. But he resolved to stop

Dreyson from talking about God. As he joined Dreyson in the living room, I listened intently to their conversation.

"Dreyson, I just talked to your dad," Cameron announced. "You need to stop talking to me about God."

Dreyson seemed amused. "My dad never said that. He knows I could never stop talking about God. Cameron, you wouldn't even have me as a friend without God!"

"What? What do you mean?" Cameron asked.

"Cameron, I almost died when I was a little baby. But some people came and prayed for me, and God answered their prayers. He healed me. If it weren't for God, I would've died."

Cameron's tone of voice quickly changed. "I didn't know *that*," he said.

"Wait here," Dreyson said as he left the room to find his proof. I peeked around the corner to see what was happening. Dreyson soon returned with pictures in his hand.

"This is what I looked like when I was a baby in the hospital," he said.

Cameron was stunned by the photos, which revealed a thin, sickly baby with tubes connected to almost every part of his little body.

"That's you?" he asked as he compared the photo with his robust friend standing next to him.

"Wow! That's amazing! You were *really* tiny. How did you get so big?"

"That's what I'm trying to tell you," Dreyson replied. "God saved my life and made me healthy."

"I didn't know *God* did that," Cameron said, sounding unsure of his own disbelief in God.

"That's not all God's done, Cameron," Dreyson responded. "He also created the world, the mountains, the ocean, outer space, and all the planets and stars." Dreyson then continued talking about the reality of God with Cameron in ten-year-old terms.

Cameron's opposition began diminishing from that day forward, and months later Dreyson confirmed that Cameron had become a believer in God.

The Fifth Gospel

What changed Cameron's mind-set about God? Dreyson's story. Dreyson could have presented Cameron with an assortment of facts and arguments proving the existence of God. But instead, he simply told his story—complete with before-and-after photos.

Christian apologetics certainly have their place. But "building a case" can prompt potential learners to stop listening and begin quickly putting up their defensive walls. Stories, on the other hand, are relational and offer great opportunities for unintimidating heart and value exchanges. They neutralize people's natural defenses and invite them to consider the possibilities of a God who loves them and desires to play the central role in their lives.

Your story is a real-life example of God's personal love and care. It broadcasts His available help and His life-changing intervention for us all.

Your story is powerful because it reflects and expresses His story.

People easily argue over logic and information. They want to debate what the truth is—and quite often the debate gets personal. In the end, no one cares how fervently you believe in your point.

But no one can argue with your story.

They can't argue that the change in your life or help God has given you isn't true—especially if they've been around you long enough to see for themselves. God's ongoing transformation in your life gives you the opportunity to tell them *why* it's true.

Some people say that five gospels have been written: Matthew, Mark, Luke, John, and You. All five are jam-packed with stories of changed lives. But of the five, *yours* is the foremost gospel that people in your sphere of influence will read.

You will live out the text of your life in the mainstream of their lives, just as Jesus lived out the text of His life in the mainstream of people's lives in His day. John explained in his gospel that, in Jesus, the Word became flesh (John 1:14). In other words, Jesus embodied the walking, breathing expression of God's Truth. Maybe that's why so much of His recorded ministry was *acted* out rather than just *preached* out.

In a sense, the same can be said of your life. Obviously, you don't live out God's Truth to the measure of perfection as Jesus did. We are always reading each other's lives—watching and learning by what we see. Our lives are like books that inform, teach, and reveal truth. Your life *is* a living testimonial of what God wants to do in the lives of others. And it may be the only "book" about Jesus they read … for a while.

You may be saying, "But, Dwight, I don't have any exciting stories to tell. What stories from my life can change someone else's life?"

You might be surprised.

Right now, would you take a moment to reflect on the stories that make up the unfolding book of your life? You might even want to exercise the helpful discipline of writing them down somewhere.

With pen and paper (or at your computer screen) begin listing your life stories using the following questions:

- What have been the spiritual turning points in your life—when God used a circumstance or life event to turn you toward Him?
- When did God unexpectedly show up for you? Surprise you?
- When has God turned something painful in your life into something good?
- How has God changed you? How are you different because of Him?
- How has God helped you—or your friends and family? Those are your stories! How has He used other people to make you more like Him?

If you'll sit with a piece of paper for a moment in God's presence, He will help you remember various and forgotten pieces of your story that might help others. And while this process will benefit your future ministry of storytelling to others, it will also provoke deep thanksgiving and worship as you recall all the times and ways God has shown up for you and others close to you.

Taking time to reflect on your life story will better prepare you for noticing and sharing overlaps between your story and others' stories.

Being Vulnerable

Some people share only the pieces of their stories that demonstrate their strengths and show they have it all together. It's safe to share those pieces. They require no risk and do nothing to tarnish their reputation.

At times, sharing your success stories is beneficial. But they comprise only a *part* of your life and story.

And it may not be the part that others need to hear.

People may need to hear about your failures and how God has or is redeeming them. They may need to hear about your pain and how God is comforting and healing you. People may need to hear about your present struggles, not your victories over past struggles. These stories often have the greatest power because they reveal the depths of your frailty and how God is still working in you.

Stories of your frailty help you establish common ground with frail people—and we're all frail people. They become starting places for you to engage in conversation with them. People think more about God when they feel afraid, insecure, uncertain, weak, and, well … frail. It allows you to enter into their need for God and let them see He's patient and kind and is still working on you.

Sharing your own pain and weakness, while not easy, can quickly open the way into deep, life-giving relationships because people see you as authentic and trustworthy.

You don't need to look far to see how God has turned the tragedies of people's life stories into ministry tools.

God turned Chuck Colson's Watergate-related prison sentence into an international ministry known as Prison Fellowship.

He turned the tragic diving accident that left Joni Eareckson

Tada a quadriplegic into Joni and Friends, an extraordinary ministry to the disabled.

And God turned the story of professional baseball pitcher Dave Dravecky, who lost his pitching arm to cancer, into a story of comfort. Through his painful story, he honors God and helps others who are facing cancer, pain, or loss.

All three of these people chose to offer God their less-than-beautiful stories to impact the lives of others. If God can use their tragedies on a national scale, could He not also use yours on a more local scale—in the life of one person at a time, in your sphere of influence?

He not only *can,* but according to Scripture, He *wants* to.

> Praise be to the … God of all comfort, who comforts us in all our troubles, so that we can comfort those in any trouble with the comfort we ourselves have received from God. For just as the sufferings of Christ flow over into our lives, so also through Christ our comfort overflows. (2 Corinthians 1:3–5)

God wants *you* to comfort others with the comfort you've received from Him.

Just like Dawn did with Diana.

Part Two
THE POWER

God's Plan A is to
express His love and power
to the world through
His Kingdom laborers.
He's the Power Source, and
His laborers are His connectors.

Eleven
Having an Acorn Outlook

The next time you see an acorn lying on the ground, pick it up. Notice how small and insignificant it looks. Then think for a moment about the *possibility* you're holding in your hand.

An acorn—a little more than an inch in diameter—holds the potential of growing into an oak tree more than one hundred feet tall, living up to a thousand years, and spawning an entire forest of other oak trees. What incredible potential that tiny acorn has!

Like an acorn, we have far more capability than what first meets the eye. God fills each life with mighty possibilities. Even the most ordinary person has extraordinary potential. In fact, I've come to believe that God delights in turning acorn-sized lives into mighty oak trees.

Just consider these "acorns" in Scripture who grew into mighty oaks:

People saw a Hebrew fugitive, but God saw a leader who would liberate Israel.

People saw a young shepherd boy, but God saw a great king.

People saw a dishonest tax collector, but God saw an accountant who eventually produced a powerful gospel account of Jesus' life.

People saw two brothers working as ordinary fishermen, but God saw fishers of men who later launched His spiritual movement.

People saw a murderer of Christians, but God saw an extraordinary missionary who would spread His church into the world.

People saw Moses, David, Matthew, Peter and Andrew, and Paul as acorns, but God saw past their appearances and shortcomings and made them into strong oak trees.

When God looks at your acorn-sized life, He sees a mighty oak tree. He doesn't see you as you are right now, but who you can become through Him. Why? Because He knows what He can do through you.

God Loves Using the Foolish, Weak, Lowly, and Despised

Jesus made a big deal out of little things. In what people minimized or overlooked, He saw great value and power.

He emphasized the importance of the widow's mite—a seemingly insignificant offering—noting the enormous size of the gift (Luke 21:1–4).

He said faith as tiny as a mustard seed held the power to move mountains (Matthew 17:20).

He explained that just a little bit of yeast affects the whole batch of dough (Matthew 13:33; Galatians 5:9).

He told a parable about the shepherd who left his flock of ninety-nine to find his one lost—but priceless—sheep (Luke 15:3–7).

And He shared another parable about a little lost coin, so valuable to its owner that when she found it, she threw a party (Luke 15:8–10).

Jesus' brother James also made a big deal about the power of little things: A tiny bit guides a strong horse; a little rudder steers a big ship; a minute spark can start a raging fire; and a small tongue can corrupt a whole person (James 3).

Paul explained how God uses little things to accomplish big things too: "God chose the *foolish* things of the world to shame the wise; God chose the *weak* things of the world to shame the strong. He chose the *lowly* things of this world and the *despised* things—and the things that are not—to nullify the things that are, so that no one may boast before him" (1 Corinthians 1:27–29).

Have you ever felt foolish or weak or lowly or despised? Then take a second look at the passage. What a happy surprise! You're exactly the kind of person God has a history of using. You're the kind of person *He chooses* to exhibit His power through. The good news—no, the great news!—is that your weaknesses and fears do not disqualify you from ministry service. Nor did they disqualify the foolish, weak, or lowly biblical heroes of the faith.

In fact, your weakness may actually qualify you for Kingdom service. Jesus said to Paul—and to us, "My power is made perfect in weakness" (2 Corinthians 12:9).

Someone once asked missionary Hudson Taylor why he thought God chose him to accomplish such a great work in China. His answer may surprise you.

"God was looking for the weakest person," he said. "And that just happened to be me."

Satan wants to paralyze you by making you feel small, as if you have nothing to offer God or His Kingdom. Don't buy into his lie.

Remember, God doesn't have a Plan B. He has called you and desires to empower you to be His Plan A to the people He has placed in your life.

Weak and lowly people really do make a difference in God's Kingdom. For proof, you don't need to look any further than a little old woman named Clenna Slater.

Church Never Tasted So Good

When I was five years old, my father pastored a small country church in rural Pennsylvania. It was a classic one-room, whitewashed church with a steeple—the kind you see in old photographs and paintings.

A beautiful sheep-grazing pasture lined one side, and a small, stately cemetery with large trees lined the other. It even had an outhouse in the back.

A single wood-burning stove, located a quarter of the way to the front of the room, heated the building. My mom sat our family close to the furnace on cold winter days so we could stay warm. That meant we sat toward the front on Sundays, which brought on some problems.

You see, I was an overactive kid—I simply could not sit still very long on those hard wooden pews. Adding insult to injury, our Sunday "church hour" was not at all kid friendly, which made it even worse for an antsy kid like me. Sitting still for even a minute seemed like an hour. Because we sat in the front of the room, everyone could see when I started getting fidgety. I was a distracting spectacle every week.

One Sunday after church, an elderly woman from the congregation approached my mom. She had gray hair and a black old-fashioned purse with a single clasp on the top.

"Does your son like peanut butter?" she asked my mom.

She was referring to me, of course, and I knew it. I listened intently as my mother replied, "Yes, he likes it a lot."

"Good," the woman continued. "I have an idea for next Sunday. See me before church begins."

The next Sunday, just before the worship service started, she approached my mother in the coatroom behind the sanctuary. We were running a little late, so the exchange was quick. She opened the clasp of her purse and pulled out a peanut butter sandwich wrapped in tinfoil.

"This is for Dwight," she instructed my mother. "It's Jif peanut butter on Wonder bread. I've cut it into four pieces so you can give him one piece every fifteen minutes to keep him occupied through the service."

Have you ever eaten peanut butter on Wonder bread? It tastes great, but it also requires a great deal of effort to un-cling the sandwich from the roof of your mouth. Clenna Slater's experiment didn't totally fill the church hour for me, but it came pretty close.

I loved it. Church never tasted so good!

Nearly every Sunday after that, Clenna did the same thing. She occasionally deviated from her routine and brought me peanut butter taffy or peanut butter cookies. But something amazing began to happen: I started looking forward to Sunday mornings.

For all of my growing-up years, I called that kind, thoughtful, creative woman the Peanut Butter Lady. I didn't even know her name was Clenna Slater until I became an adult.

Looking back, her actions weren't all that profound. But at the time, they meant the world to this hyperactive little kid whom most people avoided.

Her actions had a powerful domino effect on my life, because they endeared the church to me for the first time. Before the Peanut Butter Lady came into my life, I dreaded Sunday mornings on Saturday night! But church changed for me after she started bringing me treats. I couldn't wait to get there to find out what she brought me in her old black purse.

Something else happened during those years. I actually sat still long enough to notice what was going on. I started singing the hymns. I started praying when everyone else prayed. And I started listening to my dad's messages. I also remember feeling the presence of God for the first time in that little church. And my earliest memories of loving music were nurtured there.

It started feeling like a place where I belonged.

As I got older, I looked forward to gathering with God's people. I became heavily involved in a youth group, which helped me grow closer to God. And my love for the church grew so strong that I eventually became a pastor.

Clenna passed away a number of years ago, but I'm forever grateful to her. In fact, when I get to heaven, I'm going to ask where her mansion is so I can thank her. I'm not going to ask how to find Clenna Slater, though. I'm simply going to ask where the Peanut Butter Lady lives. I'm not exactly sure how all that will work in heaven, but somehow I think they'll know who I'm talking about.

One elderly woman with a heart of love, a black purse, a jar of peanut butter, and a bag of Wonder bread—that's what God first used to endear me to the church. And God did the rest, endearing me to Himself and so much more.

Clenna reminds me of a hymn we often sang in that country church: "Little Is Much, When God Is in It." Even though the language is a little dated (written in 1924), its message is profound. Here's one verse and the chorus:

Verse

Does the place you're called to labor
Seem too small and little known?
It is great if God is in it,
And He'll not forget His own.

Chorus
Little is much when God is in it!
Labor not for wealth or fame.
There's a crown—and you can win it,
If you go in Jesus' Name.

It's a Small World After All

A few years ago, after I spoke about Plan A at a church, a college basketball coach named Mike told me he nearly stood up on his seat and shouted, "Hallelujah!" when I said that God wants to empower *his* ministry.

"I've always felt that my 'mission field' is on a basketball court with twelve kids at a time," Mike the Basketball Coach enthusiastically exclaimed to me. "But my role in God's Kingdom has always felt little to me—especially when I compare it to what others do. Tonight, I realized that God placed me in the lives of my players so that I could bring Him up close to them. What I do may be small in others' eyes, but not in God's eyes. He wants to employ my coaching ministry."

When you understand that God wants to empower the little actions and words of your life so that He can draw others to Him, you understand that your life has great potential. Not because *you* are great, but because *He* is.

I've surrounded myself with acorns—glass acorns, papier-mâché acorns, acorn-shaped candles, acorn-designed stationery, carved acorn bookends, acorn-embellished picture frames, an acorn-themed lampshade near my desk. Acorns are strategically located throughout our ministry headquarters. And my sweet wife even agreed to include curtains in our family room that have acorns in the tapestry.

I know, you're probably thinking, *Dwight, that's overkill. No one needs that many reminders!* Yeah, well, maybe you don't. But I will always cherish nature's simple reminder that our "small" lives and moments might not be so small.

Perhaps you struggle with feelings of acorn smallness—feeling foolish, weak, lowly, or inadequate. Now is the time to stop Satan from convincing you to disqualify yourself. We all need reminders (biblical ones, historical ones, contemporary ones, even reminders from nature) to steer our minds and stir our hearts toward a stronger, unwavering conviction that God specializes in using small things to achieve *big* accomplishments.

So the next time you see an acorn on the ground, pick it up and let God use it to remind you of your potential in Him.

Twelve
Fully Charged

Frank Clewer received the shock of his life when he entered a business establishment in Warrnambool, a small town in the state of Victoria on the southern coast of Australia.

He had no idea his wool sweater and synthetic nylon jacket were rubbing together—creating friction *and* an electrical charge.

Frank felt nothing. He was totally oblivious to the electrical current that was accumulating in his clothing.

People around him, however, heard a popping sound, as if firecrackers were exploding, but they couldn't figure out where the sound was coming from. Frank heard the sounds as well, but even *he* was unaware that they were coming from him.

After taking care of his business, Frank left the building. But the people inside began smelling smoke—as if an electrical fire had started somewhere. Then they noticed smoldering, melted spots on the carpet.

Suddenly, one spot burst into flames. Startled employees called the fire department.

Firefighters arrived within minutes and immediately evacuated everyone and turned off the electricity. They suspected a power surge.

A few minutes later, as Frank stepped into his car, he noticed the smell of smoke as well—it was rising from the floor of his car. He looked down and was shocked to see the that plastic floor mat had melted beneath his foot. Jumping out of the car, he ran to get help from the firefighters who were walking outside the building.

Immediately, someone made a connection between the two: Frank was the source of the instantaneous smoldering in both his car *and* the building.

Firefighters placed a static-electricity field meter on his clothing to measure the amount of electricity he was carrying. To their amazement, he had unknowingly generated nearly 40,000 volts of static electricity!

A fire official later commented to a news agency that Frank was dangerously close to spontaneous combustion!

Something More Powerful Than 40,000 Volts

News outlets all over the world reported this story on September 17, 2005. When I first heard it, I was utterly amazed. How could a guy walk around for that long carrying that much power and not be aware of it? I couldn't fathom it.

But then I realized it happens to many of us all the time—but in a different way than it happened to Frank Clewer.

Christians like you and me walk around with God's amazing presence and transformational power at work within us, and we're often not even aware of it.

> Now to him who is able to do immeasurably more than all we ask or imagine, *according to his power that is at work within us*. (Ephesians 3:20)

> I pray also that the eyes of your heart may be enlightened in order that you may know … *his incomparably great power for us who believe*. That power is like the working of

> his mighty strength, which he exerted in Christ when he raised him from the dead and seated him at his right hand in the heavenly realms. (Ephesians 1:18–20)

The same power that raised Christ from the dead resides in us. That's more amazing than Frank's 40,000 volts! And it explains why ordinary people like you and me can have an extraordinary influence on the lives of others—because God works *in* us and *through* us.

No wonder Paul told us to "be filled" with God's Spirit (Ephesians 5:18). The greater freedom He has to work in you, the greater freedom He has to work through you. John the Baptist led the way when he said, "He must become greater; I must become less" (John 3:30). Why is this prayer so important to pray? Because you're not the *source* of the power. You're the *conductor*.

Think of yourself as a carrier of 40,000 volts of God's hope, 40,000 volts of God's love, 40,000 volts of God's wisdom, 40,000 volts of God's life-changing truth, and 40,000 volts of God's transformational power to the world around you.

And best of all, this is a renewable energy Source.

Out of your innermost being, rivers of Living Water can flow! This is God's idea—His plan—and His promise!

Source of the Power

After Jesus' resurrection, God's Plan A for ordinary people became clear. The book of Acts tells us that the Jewish religious leaders were greatly disturbed because Peter and John were preaching with power about the death and resurrection of Jesus. Many believed their message and joined their new movement.

So the Jewish leaders arrested Peter and John and asked them, "By what power or what name did you do this?" (Acts 4:7).

The leaders knew the law very well. But they weren't familiar with the spiritual power they saw in the words and actions of these two regular guys. Who or what gave these normal men such power and authority? It didn't take them long to figure out the answer to their question: "When they saw the courage of Peter and John and realized that they were *unschooled, ordinary men,* they were astonished and they took note that *these men had been with Jesus*" (Acts 4:13).

The Jewish leaders were astonished because Peter and John hadn't been trained in the top rabbinical schools of the day. No one important knew them, nor were they part of the religious elite. And yet, they clearly spoke with power and authority.

Where did their power come from?

Jesus.

Peter and John's courage and power resulted from consistently hanging out with Jesus. And ordinary men and women find supernatural courage and power today by following their example.

Years ago, fast-food restaurants began asking their customers, "Do you want to supersize your order?" They were offering a way for the customer to get far more for their money (while making a little more money for the restaurant, too).

Well, a fantastic offer is waiting for you. God's Plan A begs the question, "Do you want to supersize your life impact?"

For the earliest followers of Jesus, their answer was "Yes!"

What's your answer?

Do you want to be a container that draws upon a Source of unlimited supply? Or would you rather depend on inferior alternative forms of power? It's an easy mistake to make. But nothing can substitute for trusting in God.

We trust in the power of money.

We trust in the power of education.

We trust in the power of organizational effort.

We trust in the power of strong leadership.

We trust in the power of this world's wisdom.

And we often trust in our own power to get things done.

But God has called us to trust in *His* awesome power—and nothing else.

> Our gospel came to you not simply with words, but also with power, with the Holy Spirit and with deep conviction. (1 Thessalonians 1:5)

> If anyone speaks, he should do it as one speaking the very words of God. If anyone serves, he should do it with the strength God provides, so that in all things God may be praised through Jesus Christ. (1 Peter 4:11)

Don't Let People's Opinions Render You Powerless

Young David didn't experience the intervention of God's power until he stepped forward to defend God's reputation. Goliath, the defiant Philistine giant, had defamed the glory of God's name and honor, which filled David with true righteous indignation.

Although he had honed his sharpshooting skills while watching his father's sheep, he needed more power than his own talent could provide.

Fortunately, he chose to trust in Someone greater than Saul's weapons or armor—contrary to the advice of the people around him.

He remembered specific events from his past when he needed God to intervene on his behalf or he would have died. Because of his experience (and success) in trusting God, David knew that God's power could enable him to face sizable and formidable challenges—of the 40,000-volt size.

As you step into the challenges that accompany God's Plan A design for your life, you will likely encounter people who use your appearance and abilities as a gauge for determining what they believe is possible through you. Be careful not to listen too closely to their words.

David's brother Eliab mocked his younger brother's ability to overcome the giant standing before them. Goliath mocked David too—sneering at his youthfulness and choice of weaponry. But what Eliab, Goliath, and others didn't realize is that your potential is *limited* when you trust in yourself or other finite things. But your potential is virtually *unlimited* when you trust in God to work in and through you.

After King Saul voiced his doubts about a "boy" facing a giant, seasoned fighting machine, young David confidently replied, "The LORD who delivered me from the paw of the lion and the paw of the bear will deliver me from the hand of this Philistine" (1 Samuel 17:37). He trusted in God's power.

Recognizing David's confidence in God, Saul said, "Go, and the LORD be with you."

Throughout the Bible and Christian history we find countless examples of God's power made perfect in weak vessels—placing the Power, not the vessel, on display.

The prophet Jeremiah paints a bleak picture of what our lives look like when we trust in man, rather than in God's power.

> Cursed is the one who trusts in man, who depends on flesh for his strength and whose heart turns away from the LORD. He will be like a bush in the wastelands; he will not see prosperity when it comes. (Jeremiah 17:5–6)

Not a pretty picture, is it?

But wait. Look at the picture God paints of our lives when we trust in Him.

> But blessed is the man who trusts in the LORD, whose confidence is in him. He will be like a tree planted by the water that sends out its roots by the stream. It does not fear when heat comes; its leaves are always green. It has no worries in a year of drought and never fails to bear fruit. (Jeremiah 17:7–8)

What a difference between these two pictures!

If you feel more like a bush in the wasteland than a tree that never fails to bear fruit, there may be a good reason.

You may be depending on the flesh and living your life according to what you can see.

Perhaps, in the interest of living safe, you make choices that fail to take into consideration that God, the Creator of the universe, the

One who raised Jesus from the dead with resurrection power, lives in you.

Like Frank Clewer, you may be walking around in life with 40,000 volts of untapped power.

And you probably don't even know it.

Thirteen
Connectors

My friend David and I hadn't seen each other in quite some time. So when he extended an invitation for me to come and speak at a summer camp he was directing, I was energized to know it would enable me to speak to some youth *and* catch up with my good friend once again.

While David and I were talking in front of the concession trailer one afternoon at the camp, I noticed a shift in his focus. I was sharing some sensitive details about my life, but David stopped looking at me and fixed his eyes on something behind me.

I continued telling my story, waiting for a response and trying to regain his attention.

I spoke louder. No response. I spoke more intensely. Still no response. Nothing seemed to divert his focus. What could possibly be so enthralling?

Suddenly, David's face turned white. He jumped to his feet and frantically bolted past me. As I turned around, I understood what had distracted him.

An unsupervised little boy had been playing dangerously close to some electrical wires that were improperly connected to the concession trailer. David was watching the boy, fearing something awful might happen—and it did.

At that tragic moment, the little boy accidentally grabbed a live wire, shooting a powerful electrical current throughout his body. So strong was the current that the boy's hands were caught in its pulsating, paralyzing grip. Within moments he could be dead.

David, the only one who saw what happened, sprinted toward the helpless little boy.

The situation demanded quick thinking. Electricity was flowing through the boy's quivering body. David knew that if he tried to pull him free, the electricity could easily travel straight through the boy's body to his; so instead, he threw his body weight against the small boy and knocked him to the ground, away from the power line's grasp, saving the boy's life.

Obviously humans are not intended to be conductors of electrical force coming from a power source. We are created to be conductors of something else, something far greater, something life giving. All of us are surrounded by people desperately needing the surges of God's love, mercy, help, and blessing. We desperately need to tap into our unlimited Power Source in order to be His conductors of *love, wisdom,* and *power* to the people around us.

Your Greatest Gift

God is constantly looking for willing people to be His connectors to the world.

Here's the deal, though: To be a true and powerful connector, you must first touch the heart of God, our divine Power Source. The good news is that He wants you to touch His heart. He promises that if you come near to Him, He'll come near to you (James 4:8). If you make the effort, He'll ensure you make the connection.

The connection I'm referring to lies beyond information about God (which is good) or even giving your heart to Him through His

Son, Jesus (which is even better). What I'm referring to is intimacy (which is best): knowing God's heart and pursuing heart-to-heart exchanges with Him.

As you continually pursue deeper intimacy with God, you'll naturally experience an increase of His presence in your life. And the more you experience His presence, the greater His power will flow through you to others.

That's why I believe with all my heart that *the greatest gift you'll ever give the world is your intimacy with God.*

The more time you spend with Him, the more you'll see Him show up in your everyday life—in your home, your workplace, your church, your school, and everywhere else you go.

God intentionally gave you wonderful talents and spiritual gifts so that you'll share them with others. But people need more than you and your gifts.

They need a connection with God—His presence, power, and love.

No wonder God asks, "Who will devote himself to be close to me?" (Jeremiah 30:21).

Because as great as you are, God has far *more* to offer and wants to do so—through you:

God's thoughts and ways are much higher than yours (Isaiah 55:8–9).

His infinite love far surpasses your finite capacity to love (1 John 4:9–10).

His foolishness and weakness are far greater than your wisdom and strength (1 Corinthians 1:25).

He is the light that pierces the darkness; at best, you reflect His light (John 1:4–5, 9).

Your words can bring hope to the world, but He *is* the hope of the world (Colossians 1:27; 1 Timothy 1:1).

That's why your intimacy with God is the greatest gift you can give. He has far more to give than you do. Your supply is limited. His is endless.

You Can Do the Laborer's L

When I speak to groups about intimacy with God, I ask them do a little activity that helps them visualize their role as God's connectors to the world. Although this might seem strange, I invite you to act this out. If you don't try it, at least picture it in your mind.

Stretch your right arm into the air—straight up—as if you're reaching toward heaven. Then, stretch your left arm straight out in front of you, as if you're reaching for someone.

You should now be forming an L with your arms.

If you're doing this with me (in reality or in your imagination), you've just given yourself a visual of the kind of connector God desires you to be. With one arm reaching up to God and the other arm reaching out toward others, what's in between? You. You're the L connector between the two.

That's really what Jesus modeled for us—incredible love for His Father in heaven and deep love for people He touched every day. He was the connection between the two.

He was "love in the middle."

Now take this activity one step further. Stand up and stretch your right hand as high as it will go toward heaven—stretch until your muscles strain. Now stretch even higher. Now higher!

Often when I ask audiences to do this, some of the more

adventurous ones stand on their chairs to reach their right hands as high as they can go.

This is a visual of your relationship with God.

People hungry for God stretch and sacrifice to get as close to Him as possible.

They refuse to measure their reach toward God by the halfhearted, dispassionate attempts of so many others. Instead, they tend to read about the men and women of old whose hearts were on fire for God … and then emulate them. Following in the footsteps of those firebrand saints, they "stand on chairs" when it comes to reaching for God. They receive the reward of deeper, more powerful connections.

And as God sets their hearts ablaze, they offer a warmer and more passionate love to others.

They become "love in the middle" as they passionately stretch toward God and then stretch out to love and bless others.

You Can't Give What You Don't Have

The closer to God you get, the more of God you'll give. But the further away from God you get, the less of God (and the more of you) you'll give to others.

You can't transmit measures of God to others that you haven't received yourself. You can provide information only. But this world's great need is for power-line connectors who bring the living God's presence to life's everyday scenes.

In the book of Acts, Peter and John were walking to the temple to pray. A crippled man at the gate asked them for money, and Peter replied, "Silver or gold I do not have, but what I have I give you. In the name of Jesus Christ of Nazareth, walk" (Acts 3:6).

Peter's words are saying *you can't give what you don't have.* Peter and John couldn't give the beggar money because they had none. Likewise, you can't share God's presence with others if you're not experiencing intimacy with Him yourself.

You can try faking it or attempting a counterfeit (an empty shell with no filling) that lacks the power of God's intimate presence. You can *appear* spiritual in the eyes of others.

But if you're not close to God, you can scarcely bring Him close to others.

While on earth, Jesus spent intimate time connecting with His Father in heaven. Even He needed to touch the Power Source. The Bible tells us He often escaped to quiet places to be with His Father for extended periods of time (Mark 1:35; Luke 6:12).

To extend the Kingdom of God according to His heavenly Father's desires, Jesus needed connection time with His heavenly Father. In the same way, we need connection time with Him.

Remaining Connected

If your childhood was similar to mine, you likely played a game called Red Rover. The game involves two lines of people facing each other from about thirty feet apart. Holding hands as tightly as possible, one team calls out a runner's name from the opposing team: "Red rover, red rover, send Johnny right over."

The called person runs as hard as possible toward any potential weak link in the opposing line. The objective is to break the handheld connection and then return to the home team with the people whose hands had broken loose.

I enjoyed this game but can remember at times holding my

partners' hands so tightly that they complained. I was deeply committed to maintaining my connection (and my place on our team).

Jesus pictorially explained the importance of being connected with Him by comparing Himself to a vine and us to His branches. He declared that apart from an unbroken connection with Him, we cannot bear fruit any more than a branch can bear fruit when it's been severed from the tree.

> No branch can bear fruit by itself; it must remain in the vine. Neither can you bear fruit unless you remain in me. I am the vine; you are the branches. If a man remains in me and I in him, he will bear much fruit; apart from me you can do nothing. (John 15:4–5)

Jesus promises if you do your part and stay connected (remain in Him), He'll do His part and bear spiritual fruit through you. Not just a little fruit. He promises you'll bear much fruit!

Wow—this being true, hold on to Him for dear life! Because Jesus also said apart from a connection with Him, you'll produce no fruit. None.

Now be aware that you may think you're seeing results—and your results may look like "fruit." But if your efforts are just *your* efforts and not a result of what flows from Him, then your "results" are no different from the bowl of fruit sitting on my family-room coffee table. The bowl of fruit may look lovely—in fact, it looks perfect—but try taking a bite. Very quickly you'll discover it's made of plastic. Fake fruit looks good, but it serves as a poor substitute for the real deal.

Recently, while driving in my neighborhood, I noticed a large branch hanging down from a beautiful plum tree. It was still connected but hanging only by a small piece of bark. The branch was completely separated from its life source, and sadly, I knew it was dying.

As beautiful as the limb had once been, it would no longer produce fruit. Apart from the tree, it could do nothing.

I went home to retrieve my trimmers and soon returned to cut off the remaining piece of bark. With one snip, the limb fell to the ground.

The weighted truth this poignant image provided made me feel sick. You and I can add matchless beauty and produce much fruit when we're connected to the Source of life. But when we're no longer connected to our Source, we're powerless, fruitless, lifeless, and in need of being pruned.

Are you connected to the Vine? Are you bearing fruit? Or are you hanging by a thread of bark? To fulfill God's Plan A for your life, to bear *much* fruit, you must remain in Him.

When I stooped down to pick up the severed branch on the ground, my thoughts drifted to my ever-tight-grip connections while playing Red Rover at school. And I wondered what grand possibilities exist for those who hold on tightly to God and simply let His power and life flow through them.

Fourteen
Along the Way

In 2008, the Christian big band Denver & the Mile High Orchestra placed third in the Fox Network television show *The Next Great American Band.*

Apart from the fact that Denver Bierman, the band's lead singer, is a longtime friend, my kids and I love listening to the band's music. But more than their broad appeal, I appreciate their love for God and the way they point people to Him through their music.

Four years before their television appearances, our family attended one of their concerts. Midway through the evening, Denver shared that the band hoped to perform free, open-air, evangelistic concerts at the upcoming 2004 Olympic Games in Athens, Greece.

At that point, just four months before the trip, they were still $50,000 short of the necessary funds. After his appeal, he gave the audience an opportunity to give toward the band's summer ministry tour.

Immediately, I caught the vision. I knew their high-energy, twelve-piece band would be perfect for drawing and keeping crowds.

What I didn't know was that my twelve-year-old daughter, Dara, caught the vision too. During Denver's appeal, God spoke to her about the money she'd been saving for over a year to buy a small motor scooter. He wanted her to give it to the band instead.

During the second half of the concert, Dara approached her mom and me and shared what God was asking her to do.

"Would you be willing to write a check for the entire amount I have in my savings account?" she asked. "I promise to pay you back tomorrow."

We questioned Dara to make sure she was certain this was from God. She was.

"I feel *very* clear that this is what God wants me to do," she assured us.

Then we questioned her again to make sure *we* were certain. We were. So we wrote the check.

After the concert, Denver heard about Dara. Not only did her generosity encourage and deeply move him, but he was also convinced it would serve as the "loaves and fishes" God would use to provide for their trip.

A few months later, Denver & the Mile High Orchestra traveled to the Athens Olympics and shared its music with thousands of people from all over the world. After their concerts, the band members built relationships with people who listened to their music.

They shared Christ with many unbelievers and encouraged several Christians from Islamic countries who had fled religious persecution in their homeland.

And Dara? She started saving for that scooter again. She knew she wouldn't have enough money for another year or so, and that was okay by her. She was thrilled to play a role in sending the gospel to another nation through one of her favorite bands.

I was thrilled that Dara experienced her first taste of Spirit-directed living and laboring—and it was a good taste. Even as a young girl, she was discovering that God *wants* to speak to her and guide her.

God wants the same for all of us. He wants to interact with

us throughout the day—regardless of where we are or what we're doing—even apart from special alone times we spend with Him and His Word.

Jesus, the Good Shepherd, said that His followers follow His lead because they know His voice (John 10:4).

It's His job to lead; it's our job to listen and obey.

Our obedience to His "in the moment" promptings matter for eternity. We may not understand at the time why He asks us to do something, but He knows. And His ways and thoughts are higher than ours (Isaiah 55:8–9).

Here's Your Hat

A friend of mine was shopping in a department store when suddenly he sensed God telling him to go to the men's area and look at the winter hats.

Once he reached the men's department, he sensed God telling him, "Buy all the winter hats in the bin in front of you!"

"Dwight, it was absolutely the strangest sensation—so strong and so weird. You know I'm a regular guy, and my mental faculties are in place," he later told me. "My eyes bugged right out of my head as I sensed God's presence. I thought perhaps other people could hear Him speaking too." He chuckled. "Fortunately all the hats were on sale!"

Rolling his cart up to the cash register and beginning to unload his basket, the store clerk paused, wrinkled her forehead, and then looked at him. "What are you going to do with all of these hats?"

"I don't know," he said, laughing. At that point, all he knew was that God told him to buy the hats and that something strange was in the works.

The clerk laughed too, saying this was her most unusual and memorable purchase ever. My friend smiled, confirming it was his most unusual purchase in his lifetime of shopping. Perhaps trying to make him more comfortable, she mentioned that her husband purchased one of those hats and thought it was the warmest winter hat he'd ever owned. My friend then put all the hats (two big bags!) in the trunk of his car and nearly forgot about them.

Several weeks later while driving home from work, he rounded the bend of his street and headed for his cul-de-sac when he encountered what looked like a garbage-truck convention—right on his street. For some reason, garbage trucks were parked everywhere, and all the garbage workers were standing outside their trucks, talking with each other. It was an extremely unusual sight.

But what made the sight even stranger was that not one of the workers was wearing a hat—and this was the coldest day of the year in Colorado.

"I quickly pulled over, opened the trunk of my car, and had fun passing out all the nice new winter hats—with the tags still on them," my friend told me as he began to weep. "To share God's love that day with those cold men was such a spiritual highlight for me."

My friend experienced what it means to be "love in the middle"—embodying God's love to others. But this privilege is not on reserve for a few.

God Is Already Speaking to You

God has given each one of us—including you—the ability to hear His voice. He doesn't limit Himself to a select group of spiritually sensitive people equipped with some kind of "direct line" to heaven.

Throughout His Word, God *promises* that He speaks to us.

> The LORD confides in those who fear him. (Psalm 25:14)
>
> Whether you turn to the right or to the left, your ears will hear a voice behind you, saying, "This is the way; walk in it" (Isaiah 30:21)
>
> I am the LORD your God, who teaches you what is best for you, who directs you in the way you should go. (Isaiah 48:17)
>
> The LORD will guide you always. (Isaiah 58:11)
>
> He who belongs to God hears what God says. (John 8:47)

It's pretty clear. God not only *wants* to speak to His people—He already is!

Unfortunately, we don't listen very well. Like children who tune out their parents' voices, we can easily tune out God's voice. Sometimes we don't hear His voice because we don't *want* to hear it—because then we'd be accountable to obey.

When my son was very young, I jokingly said, "It may be time to take you to the ear doctor." He looked panicked until I said, "Because you have so much trouble hearing what I've asked you to do." Then he looked sheepishly guilty. He knew he had some attentive adjusting to do. The same could be said of us in our relationship with God.

Sometimes our personal agendas drown out His voice. We

rush through our lives and get so busy staying on task that, without realizing it, we miss important Kingdom-advancing moments along the way.

We become experts in *tuning in* the horizontal and *tuning out* the vertical.

That's why Dawn and I didn't hesitate long in writing a check that night, enabling Dara to give away her savings. In a horizontal moment (at a concert), Dara tuned in to the vertical (she listened to God's voice). And although her request to empty her entire savings account initially concerned us, we remembered a woman in the Bible who emptied an entire bottle of expensive perfume to wash Jesus' feet in an expression of her love.

We wanted to affirm Dara's desire to give everything out of her love for God. And we wanted to reinforce her faith and belief that God speaks to each of us and calls us to act in ways we hadn't planned. Most of all, we wanted to encourage her to keep listening for God's voice.

Many of us need to change our listening habits from the horizontal stations that blare at us all day to God's vertical voice, which often comes in a still, small voice.

He speaks to us regularly and often. But we easily miss Him if we're not attentive.

God didn't speak to Elijah the prophet in the mighty wind or the earthquake or the fire. He spoke to him in a gentle whisper (1 Kings 19:11–12).

Shhh! Perhaps God is speaking to you in a gentle whisper too. As you've read this book, maybe He's been nudging you in soft and subtle ways.

Are you listening attentively? Can you hear Him? Are you taking notes as you listen? Have you written down action steps that He wants you to take? Or is your life moving too fast to hear, record, and respond to His gentle, instructional whispers?

When I think of maintaining vertical and horizontal attentiveness, I think of what martyred missionary Jim Elliot once wrote: "Wherever you are, be all there." It's become one of my favorite quotes.

His words remind me to stay in the moment—avoid getting so caught up in life's busyness that I'm unable to hear God's voice and spontaneously obey Him.

You and I have the opportunity to embrace this everyday lifestyle of Spirit-directed living and laboring as we listen for God's promptings in the moment and along the way.

Interruptions Are the Ministry

By living a Spirit-directed life, we follow the example of Jesus, who said, "My food is to do the will of Him who sent Me" (see John 4:34). Jesus' highest purpose was to fulfill the Father's agenda—not getting upset by interruptions, but embracing them as opportunities. Stopping along the way to take care of someone's immediate need was the norm of His life, not the exception. Is it yours?

Time and time again, engaged with His surroundings and the timeliness of an opportunity presenting itself, Jesus slowed down or completely stopped what He was doing to minister to someone. That's a hard model for many of us to pattern our lives after because we're more consumed by our type A personalities than we are about putting into practice God's Plan A for reaching the world.

For type A personalities (like me), hearing God's voice in the moment and stopping along the way are difficult things to do. After stating our destination, we race toward the goal—doing our best to avoid anyone or anything threatening to divert us from the quickest and most direct path to get there. We're known for our goals, plans, schedules, and sticking to them. Maybe you can relate.

But God challenges and calls us to serendipitous ministry—along the way.

He rarely operates according to *our* schedules. He often prompts us to break out of them so we can minister to others in their moment of need. Unfortunately, we tend to become so reliant upon our schedules and routines that we view His promptings as *interruptions* rather than *opportunities*. It's a selfish way to live. And it dramatically scales down our potential for high-impact Kingdom living.

A friend of mine placed this message in a prominent location on his desk: "Interruptions *are* the ministry." The first time I saw it, I asked him why it was there.

"I've noticed over the years that it's easy to lose sight of what ministry is really about," he replied. "We focus too much on tasks when ministry is ultimately about people. I need to constantly remind myself that people aren't an interruption to my work. They *are* my work."

Likewise, God's promptings aren't interruptions to your life and ministry. They're the ministry of your life … and they're the life of your ministry. They're part of God's Plan A for you.

That's why Jesus often responded to along-the-way, in-the-moment, interruptive, and Spirit-directed ministry opportunities:

- While on His way to heal a dying young girl, He noticed that a woman touched His garment and received healing (Mark 5:21–34). He slowed down, embraced the moment, and engaged in an impromptu conversation that changed her life.

- Jesus was walking to Galilee and stopped at a well to get a drink of water. There, He met a woman, but it wasn't by coincidence. More than water, she needed something to quench her spiritual thirst. Through insightful questions and words, Jesus forever impacted her life—and many others who heard about Him through this woman (John 4:4–42).

- Another time, Jesus passed through Jericho—on His way to Jerusalem—and noticed a man way up in a tree, trying to catch a glimpse of Him. Jesus realized Zacchaeus needed more than a glimpse; he needed an up-close encounter. So, Jesus asked him to come down immediately so they could hang out at his house together (Luke 19:1–10).

These weren't "planned" ministry meetings. They weren't coincidences either. Not from God's perspective. They were Spirit-directed ministry moments that brought God's Kingdom to people in need—all along the way.

Following His Cues

If Jesus paid attention to interruptions and "coincidences" along the way, it's probably safe to say He wants you to do the same.

He'll prompt you like an offstage director giving cues to an onstage actor.

He'll prompt you when He wants you to notice someone or when He wants you to slow down, stop, listen, or say something.

He'll prompt you to pray urgently for a person or need.

He'll prompt you to schedule a lunch or coffee with someone—ahead of time or in the spur of the moment.

He'll prompt you to make a phone call, text someone, or write a note. He'll even tell you what to say during your call or in the message.

He'll prompt you to place a hand on a shoulder, lend a listening ear, or simply be present with someone without saying anything at all.

It might feel like a gentle nudge inside or something in your spirit going off like a soft, beeping alarm. Your heart might beat a little stronger, or your breathing might get faster. You may feel overwhelming compassion for a person or situation and feel that you *must* do something. And sometimes you'll hear that gentle whisper. You may not always be sure if it's Him, but in the moment, learn to risk stepping out.

You'll be unsure about where it will lead, but trust the One who's leading. When God brokers a "divine appointment," you don't want to miss it.

But most exciting of all, God is *already* prompting you—whether or not you're listening. Every day, He invites you to join Him in building His Kingdom. Now, before you start beating yourself up over your missed opportunities, please understand that even the most discerning person misses plenty of "God moments." But every day, He whispers, guides, prompts, and leads us.

Learning to listen requires that we reorient our lives from the horizontal to the vertical. Actually, it requires that we take both into account. We make ourselves aware of the people and circumstances around us (even the small stuff) while listening to the promptings of the Holy Spirit.

What if We're Wrong?

When I speak to different groups about Spirit-directed ministry, people often ask me, "What if I get it wrong? What if I think I'm hearing from God, but it's really not Him, and then I do something that God didn't really prompt me to do?"

While this is a legitimate concern, a far more important concern should be that we will miss critical (maybe even urgent) in-the-moment ministry opportunities if we do nothing. In most cases, the worst that can happen if you get it wrong is possibly looking foolish to others.

I wonder how often our fear of getting it wrong or looking foolish causes us to miss out on countless opportunities to obey God and minister to others.

I'm willing to take that chance, aren't you?

However, if the consequences of getting it wrong are great, you may want to be more cautious. You may even want to seek the counsel of others. But in the end, *you* are responsible for what God speaks to you.

A dear friend of mine used to say, "God can steer a moving car far better than He can steer a car that's stuck in park." Learn to respond to God's in-the-moment, along-the-way promptings by taking action steps of obedience, rather than allowing endless internal debates to paralyze you and prevent you from joining God in critical Kingdom opportunities.

People overtly consumed with personal safety, self-protection, self-image, and self-promotion usually won't expand God's Kingdom much.

If the fear of looking foolish (a nice way of saying "prideful") prevents you from stepping out, remember Jesus in the garden of Gethsemane the night before He was nailed to a cross. He paid the price for your freedom with His life.

At the moment when He had everything to lose, He surrendered His will to the Father and prayed, "Not as I will, but as you will" (Matthew 26:39).

Don't allow the fear of being wrong or looking foolish keep you locked in park. When you listen for His voice and act on His promptings, you'll be amazed at how God drives you into Spirit-directed moments that will leave an eternal impact. Once you go down this road, you'll never want to look back!

You may get it wrong from time to time. No biggie. Practice is the only way to get better at hearing His voice.

The Rest of Dara's Story

What if Dara heard wrong? What if God *hadn't* spoken to her about sacrificially giving her savings so Denver & the Mile High Orchestra could go overseas? What if her youthful sentiments spoke to her rather than God? Seriously, what's the worst that could have happened?

As it turned out, God used Dara's sensitivity and obedience more than I would have ever imagined. Here's the rest of the story:

A few months after Dara's gift, I shared her story while preaching at a church in Indianapolis. I had never talked about it in public, and I hadn't planned on telling it in *this* message. But midway through my sermon, God repeatedly urged me to tell the story. I shared it at an appropriate place and continued preaching.

At the close of the service, a distinguished-looking businessman named Bruce approached me. Dara's act of obedience had deeply moved him.

"God spoke to me about my own personal obedience through Dara's example," Bruce the Businessman said. He went on to tell me that one of the multiple businesses he owned was a motorcycle shop. "Dwight, God prompted me to give your daughter the scooter she was saving for. I think this is a test of *my* obedience. Maybe it's the first of many."

I didn't think much about it until he called me two weeks later and asked me to go to a Web site and choose the scooter color she wanted.

We followed his instructions, and a few weeks later, the scooter arrived at my office!

God's rewards for our small acts of obedience don't always tangibly come in this life (my wife and I made that clear to Dara!). But I can't tell you how much it meant to our daughter to feel the smile of God's approval when she received a surprise blessing.

She knew He was proud of her for putting Him and His Kingdom ahead of personal gain. And she'll know for the rest of her life that God speaks in unexpected moments and in unexpected ways.

Another Amazing Sequel!

Believe it or not, Dara's story didn't end with the motor scooter. God continued to bless Dara's step of obedience.

A year later, I returned to Indianapolis, so I asked Bruce the Businessman to join me for lunch.

As we sat down to eat, I could tell Bruce wanted to share something important with me. He also brought a friend with him.

"Dwight," he began, "your story about how your daughter listened to God's voice really moved me. In fact, that's when I made a commitment to listen for His voice too. And over the past year, that change set in motion a God-led chain of events that radically altered my life, personal ministry, and my future. One by one, I've done my best to act on God's promptings … and the results have been amazing!"

Bruce then introduced me to the young man sitting next to him. Beaming, the man told me how he came to know Christ through Bruce's living testimony.

Bruce shared with me that he'd begun leading Bible studies for his employees and that a number of them made decisions to follow Jesus, which led to swimming-pool baptism services for employees, friends, and family members who'd made spiritual commitments.

Throughout all this, Bruce began sensing that God was calling him to redeem the time he'd lost—years of living for his own agenda.

Bruce couldn't contain it any longer. "God has opened doors for me to serve Him overseas," he exclaimed. "And it all began that morning when I made that first step of obedience to God's in-the-moment prompting to give a scooter to your daughter."

As Bruce spoke, I thought about the chain of events God had set in motion through ordinary laborers being obedient to His in-the-moment promptings. God used a series of simple acts of obedience and created something bigger out of them.

Denver & the Mile High Orchestra answered God's call to go to Greece. My daughter obeyed God by giving sacrificially to help them go. I obeyed God's prompting to tell her story in the middle of a message. Bruce the Businessman obeyed God, giving Dara the scooter she had been saving for.

And God continued the chain of events by using Bruce to spiritually impact his family, friends, and company—and eventually led him into overseas missions work.

Bruce the Businessman soon became Bruce the Missionary, and he's currently serving an unreached people group halfway around the world.

What could God set in motion through *your* daily acts of obedience? Are you missing the chance to set off a chain of events because you're not listening for His voice? Do you ignore His promptings because you can't imagine far enough down the road what He might want to accomplish through your obedience?

Remember, you may not understand His promptings in the moment. Dara didn't understand for a while.

A few weeks after she gave her life savings, she asked me, "Daddy, how much would it cost to get a group the size of Denver & the Mile Orchestra across the ocean on a plane?"

"A lot," I replied. I didn't want her to think her gift was small when she compared it to their great need.

But she kept asking, "How much, Dad?"

"Oh, I don't know exactly." I hoped she would let it go. She didn't.

When she discovered the total cost of their airfare, she said, "How embarrassing! My gift didn't do much."

But I quickly replied, "Honey, it wasn't the size of your gift that captured God's attention. It was the amount left over. You gave it *all!* He measures the size of your obedience, He sees your heart of willing sacrifice, and He adds His immeasurable blessings. God will use what you gave to change lives!"

Little did I know! The ripples of Dara's obedience can be felt halfway around the world. That's what God does when His Plan A Kingdom laborers commit to follow His lead in the moment … along the way.

Imagine what God's ready to do as *you* listen and obey.

Part Three

THE PROBLEM

God's Plan A is to minister through ordinary, uniquely designed, up-close, mainstream, divinely connected, along-the-way ministers. But there's a problem that challenges that plan.

Are you part of the problem?

Fifteen
The Parade

When I was nine years old, my family and I attended a parade on Main Street in my small hometown. In order to grab a choice spot along the parade route, my sister and I jumped on our bicycles and rode ahead of the rest of the family.

Like any small-town parade, the procession was very simple. It consisted of makeshift floats, men and women in thrown-together clown outfits, Boy and Girl Scout troops, civic clubs, politicians in freshly waxed cars, the high school marching band, local fire engines, and police cars.

To be honest, the whole thing wasn't that exciting until a group of my peers passed by on their decorated bicycles. *That* caught my attention.

These kids weren't just sitting on the curbside watching the parade with the rest of us. And they weren't doing anything special—just riding their bicycles. But they were *in* the parade, and I was thrilled to see that someone like me could join in.

"Mom, those are *my* friends in the parade!" I shouted.

"Do you want to join them?" she immediately replied.

"I couldn't do that!" I insisted, assuming the kids in the parade belonged to some special group. My mother knew otherwise: It was a low-budget, open-to-anyone kind of parade.

My heart pounded at the thought of actually being *in* the parade, but I continued my halfhearted protest. "Mom, my bike isn't decorated like their bikes. Mine is just plain."

"It doesn't need to be decorated," she persisted as she lifted my bike upright from the ground. "Go ahead; it's your chance! Get out there with the rest of your friends! I'll find you at the end of the parade route."

Standing right beside me, her bike in hand, was my sister. Immediately my mom began appealing for her to see this as an equal opportunity, urging her, "Hurry. You both can enter the parade route together." I joined my mother's pleading. But my sister's timidity and the speed at which the decision needed to be made took control. She froze, shying away from her chance to participate, while I looked once again at all the excitement and opportunity about to pass me by.

"Really? I can *really* do that?" I asked, looking for one final bit of reassurance.

I glanced at my father, just to be sure. He didn't need to say anything for me to tell he was concerned. I could see reservation plainly on his face.

But my mom—who's very much a risk-taking, parade kind of woman—won out. Helping to usher me and my bike through the crowd and into the street, she reassured me.

"It's okay! Hurry! You're going to miss out if you don't get in there."

Quickly I caught up with the rest of my friends and joined the parade.

For the next thirty minutes or so, I savored the too-good-to-be-true reality that I was *in* the parade! I kept glancing in disbelief at all the spectators to my left and right.

I had the time of my life.

However, despite my mom's energetic coaxing, my sister had refused to join me. She was too afraid.

My family met me at the end of the parade route, and my parents placed my bike in the trunk of the car. As we drove home, I proudly recounted every moment of the experience.

Sitting on the Sidelines

My childhood parade experience resembles the way most Christians approach life and ministry. Most people sit on the sidelines, watching the parade go by. They're content to watch others get involved while they sit in their comfortable seats at a safe distance away from the action.

One of the greatest challenges to God's Plan A for reaching the world is spectators.

Pastors often refer to the "80-20 principle" that applies to most churches. Put simply, this principle states that in most churches 80 percent of the work is done by 20 percent of the people. Maybe you've seen this principle at work in your own church.

Apparently, the harvest (ministry opportunity) is *still* plentiful, and the laborers (ministry participants) are *still* too few (Matthew 9:37).

God's Plan A for reaching the world is to mobilize every Christian (as an active laborer) into every place of human need. But how can He fulfill His plan if fewer than 20 percent of His people participate?

To put it another way, how can He fulfill His plan when more than 80 percent of His followers are spectators?

God desires to extend His grace, love, and power to so many more people in the world than currently receive it. But when He looks for willing laborers through whom He can express His will, He finds few. There just aren't enough active laborers.

The problem doesn't come from a shortage of Christians. The problem comes from a shortage of *willingness* from Christians to put their faith into action. Instead, they prefer to live as spectators—watching from the sidelines.

An Unresponsive Body

I wonder how God must feel when He sees so many human needs but so few mobilized laborers He can use to meet them. I wonder if it saddens Him, frustrates Him, angers Him.

One day as I arrived at a park for a recreational day away with our family, I caught a glimpse of how He must feel. I noticed a young military veteran in a wheelchair enjoying a day of fun with his wife and two children a short distance away from where we were picnicking.

As I occasionally observed this other father and his family, I repeatedly and painfully began witnessing the longing of this loving dad to be more physically interactive than he was able with his children. They had begun playing far beyond the reach of his wheelchair path. His heart clearly wanted to be up close—but neither his body nor wheelchair would get him there.

Suddenly, I heard a child scream and saw heartbreaking emotion erupt on this father's face. One of his children had accidentally fallen and began crying out in pain. The young father couldn't reach her to offer the comfort he so wanted to give. As I watched, he lunged forward, almost completely falling out of his wheelchair. Then his face grimaced, and in anguish he began to cry. He longed to reach out to his child—to hold her up close—but his paralyzed arms and legs made it impossible.

I was overcome with waves of sadness as I took in the agonizing scene of a longing dad's heart, a heart trapped inside a body incapable of expressing what the mind and will of this dear father wanted. Tears filled my eyes. I couldn't stop thinking about it.

How must it feel for your head to tell your body to do something but it won't? It must be more frustrating than I can imagine.

Later, I sensed Jesus telling me, "Dwight, I'll tell you how it feels." And it hit me like a ton of bricks! Jesus has a "body." And He knows all too well how it feels.

Scripture tells us Jesus is the head, and we are His body. The head continually communicates with the body. The head tells the body to go over there, say this, or do that. But what happens when the body refuses to cooperate?

Far too often, the body of Christ has failed to respond according to the will of its head. It's stuck in spectator mode.

How many times does Jesus yearn to speak words of love or encouragement to someone who is hurting or searching for answers, but *His mouth* won't respond?

He longs to be close to people across a room, across the street, or even across the world, but *His feet* won't obey—they won't go where He tells them.

Jesus once held children in His arms and blessed them. Today, He wants to continue holding and blessing children, but *His arms* fail to cooperate.

The music group Casting Crowns expressed it this way in their song "If We Are the Body":

But if we are the body

Why aren't his arms reaching?

Why aren't his hands healing?

Why aren't his feet going?

Why is his love not showing them there is a way?

Why aren't we reaching, healing, teaching, and going? Because the body isn't obeying the head.

Far too often, Jesus must feel like He lives in a quadriplegic body.

Grievous Consequences

Think about this for a moment: What are the consequences when so few people in the body actively obey Jesus? How does it affect the world?

Well, for starters, the active 20 percent in the body are prone to burnout—even though fulfilling their ministry calling should be an incredible source of joy and purpose. Why? Because they see so much need around them and try to do too much by themselves. So, they overcompensate for the inactive and unengaged remainder of Christ's body.

On the flip side, the inactive—spectating—80 percent miss out on the joy and sense of purpose that come from being involved in daily, active Kingdom service. They miss out on the incredible joy and exhilaration that come from living a life of purpose.

I have always loved the motto of famous missionary Jim Elliot: "He is no fool who gives up what he cannot keep to gain that which he cannot lose." Why spend your life aimlessly when you can invest it purposefully?

But here's the most disturbing consequence: Jesus' Plan A work doesn't get done. Broken and hurting people around the world (in workplaces and neighborhoods everywhere) who need the up-close love of Christ never receive it! Salve to their wound—Christ's love shown to them through an active laborer—might be within arm's reach. Jesus sees the need and wants to do something about it but needs His body to respond to Him, their head.

Around the world right now, offices and factories are filled with unhappy, unfulfilled employees. Schools are filled with insecure students feeling they don't measure up to their peers. Unwanted children wait for "forever families." Hungry, homeless people fill our streets. Single parents strive to raise children alone. Bars are filled with lonely, broken people trying to numb themselves against the pain around them. And our neighborhoods and apartment complexes are filled with people desperate for the kind of love manifested by those connected to the One who *is* love.

And, at the same time, our churches are filled with immobilized people who are uninvolved in the everyday lives of the very people they should (and so easily could) engage—people who need what they have.

Jesus must be frustrated and grieved by the inaction of His quadriplegic body.

A fully functioning body is critical to God's Plan A for reaching the world.

Join In!

When I picked up my bike and joined the parade years ago, I had the time of my life. My sister, on the other hand, let her fear prevent her from getting into the action.

What about you? Are you involved or sitting on the sidelines?

Are you in or out?

Here's the deal: The parade passes by only *once.* So what are you waiting for? This is your *only* chance. You can't go back and reclaim a missed opportunity.

There's no comparison between talking about the parade and being in it. Living vicariously through the lives of other parade participants doesn't come close either.

Being a spectator is not God's calling on your life! His Plan A for reaching the world requires your involvement.

Come on. Grab your bike. Join the parade!

Sixteen
In or Out?

Years ago, I served as an emcee and worship leader for a large student gathering held at the University of Illinois. It was one of the most powerful student events I've ever participated in. Over the years, hundreds of people have expressed to me that God deeply impacted their lives at that event.

Well-known author and pastor E. V. Hill served as one of the speakers. I stood backstage with Rev. Hill as a band performed the special music before he spoke. As I rehearsed in my mind what I would say to introduce him, I turned to ask him a question and noticed he was fighting back tears.

"Are you okay?" I asked, unsure if I should be interrupting him in the moment. Something was clearly moving him.

"Yes, I'm okay," he replied as he scanned the sea of young faces in the University of Illinois arena. He paused for a moment before he continued. "I get overwhelmed when I see this many young people gathered together. So many of them don't know how important they are to God—and how important they are to the work God wants to do in this world."

Rev. Hill paused again as he continued to look around the arena. "When I was their age, I didn't even think God knew who I was. I certainly didn't know that He had a plan for my life."

He explained that as an African American kid growing up in the South, he never had a vision for doing anything beyond surviving.

I thought for a moment about how far he had come.

A few moments later, Rev. Hill stood on the platform and delivered one of the most powerful sermons I have ever heard. I'm pretty sure he didn't preach what he'd planned. I think God wanted to say something to thousands of youth that night, and He found His mouthpiece in E. V. Hill.

As he began, Rev. Hill stood and again scanned the crowd in front of him. The place remained still until he broke the silence.

With his southern accent and slow, drawn-out cadence, he proclaimed, "Gawd … has … a plan … for you."

He repeated the phrase.

"Gawd … has … a plan … for you … and you … and you … and you," he said as he pointed at different young people in the audience.

"It ain't your mama's plan. And it ain't your daddy's plan." The crowd laughed, and some individuals actually looked relieved.

"It's God's one-and-only plan for you," he said and then paused again for dramatic effect.

"And there ain't no Plan B."

"You're it! … You're it! … You're it!"

I was mesmerized and deeply impacted by the powerful message he delivered that night. I never forgot his frequent use of the phrase "There ain't no Plan B." Subsequently I found myself deducing, *That's it! There is a Plan A! We need to recover, rediscover, rekindle, revive, and restore the one and only original plan—the one Jesus modeled. Because it's not* a *plan, it's* the *plan. The God-designed plan He has for each one of us should be called "Plan A."*

Rev. Hill ended the message by inviting everyone in the audience to respond to God's plan for them. Thousands came forward that night to say "I'm in."

Don't Buy Into the Lie

Hopefully by now you've decided that you're "all in" too. If you are, then be aware—your enemy, Satan, wants to get you back out.

And if you aren't committed to being all in, it may be the result of Satan working hard to keep you out.

When you commit to being all in for God's purposes in your life, you become a threat to Satan. He knows that when you leave the sidelines and become a connector of God's love in the mainstream of life, your impact multiplies and spreads far beyond your limited sphere of influence.

Satan knows that as you remain in the Vine, you bear much fruit. And he knows that as you allow God to lead and empower you in the moment and along the way, you expand the boundaries of God's Kingdom on earth. Expect Satan to fight against the daily activation of God's Plan A in your life. He wants to prevent you from being "all in."

Not only does God have a plan for your life, but Satan does too. He wants you stuck on the sidelines—uninvolved in Kingdom service. And he'll do whatever he can to discourage you or recycle you so you return to "inactive" status. He'll even try to convince you that you're doing God a favor by staying out of the race. His plans for your life include disqualifying yourself because you aren't a good-enough Christian. He even wants you thinking that qualified people exist—you just aren't one of them.

Satan is a deceiver, and he knows how to play with your mind. He knows how to discourage you with thoughts about your life that run counter to God's. He tries to sow seeds of doubt in your mind so you prohibit yourself from living out God's purposes. If he can get you to disqualify yourself, he knows you'll remain in spectator mode.

Here are some of the lies Satan uses to keep you missing in action.

Lie #1: "I'm not perfect enough."

Think for a moment. How many people do you know who are perfect? I'm not referring to people who *think* they're perfect. How many truly perfect people do you know? None, of course.

There are no perfect people.

Of course, you already know this. You probably offer this morsel of truth to comfort others when they make mistakes. Yet, if you're like many people, you hesitate and disqualify yourself from God's Plan A Kingdom service because of your repeated battles with frailty and imperfection. You convince yourself that God has laborers at His disposal much less flawed than you.

Not true!

But you've pressed Rewind and listened to this lie so many times that you don't even realize how much it affects you. *I'm not good enough or perfect enough for God to really use me,* you rehearse to yourself.

With the utmost confidence, I promise that this self-imposed verdict contradicts God's verdict for your life. How do I know? Because God has always included greatly flawed people in His plan. In fact, they are the only people He works with.

The great heroes of the Bible were as flawed as you and me. Reread your favorite passages about Noah, Abraham, Sarah, Jacob, Moses, Rahab, Gideon, David, the disciples, and others—only this time, notice how God used them *despite* their major flaws.

God doesn't have a Plan B. Imperfect people are *the key* to His plan. Your imperfections in no way diminish His desire to use you. Since the beginning of time, God has had only one perfect person at His disposal through whom He could work: Jesus. Otherwise, for thousands of years He's used imperfect "earthen vessels" to show His all-surpassing power.

We need to stop waiting for some undetermined day in the future when we foolishly think we'll be closer to being perfect—or better than we are now—before we accept God's Plan A assignments for our lives.

By the time you *are* perfect—when you see God face-to-face in heaven and you're changed into His likeness—you'll be of no more earthly value to Him. By that point, you've already missed your opportunity to be God's Plan A.

Just do what John the Baptist did. He didn't claim to be perfect, but he called attention to the only One who is. He *pointed* people to Jesus and said, "Look, the Lamb of God, who takes away the sin of the world! … I have seen and I testify that this is the Son of God" (John 1:29, 34).

You don't need to be perfect to be a pointer. You just need to be willing to redirect the focus off yourself and on to Him.

When you get over yourself and lift your gaze toward Him, others will too.

Lie #2: "I'm not worthy."

We rarely say this, but many of us feel it. The Enemy has ingrained the "I'm not worthy" lie so deeply into our minds that many of us actually start believing we're doing the right thing by *not* getting involved in ministry service. We're simply not worthy enough to take part in something so important.

We feel unworthy because we've done something bad or something bad has been done to us. As a result, we feel like damaged goods. We fail to see our own value, and we can't imagine that God sees it either.

But the Bible clearly tells us that we mean the world to Him: For God so loved the world that He sent Jesus to save us (John 3:16). In fact, our worth hasn't changed since the day we were born. Regardless of what we've done or what's been done to us, we still hold great value to God.

When I speak at Plan A conferences, I often pull out a crisp twenty-dollar bill, hold it up, and ask if anyone wants it. Every time, a number of hands shoot up in the air. They're thinking, *Who wouldn't want a twenty-dollar bill?*

"Wait a minute," I say to them as I crumple up the bill in my hand until it's in a tight little ball.

Then I hold up the little ball and ask, "Now who wants it?"

Even more hands shoot up into the air.

"Okay, wait another minute," I say to them as I drop the bill and grind it into the dirty floor with my shoe.

I reach down, pick it up, and raise it back into the air. It's now a very wrinkled and dirty twenty-dollar bill.

"Now who wants it?" I ask. And without exception, even more hands go up. Some even start shouting, "I want it!"

Why would so many people want a wrinkled, soiled twenty-dollar bill? Because it hasn't lost its value.

And neither have you.

Regardless of your past or present, your great value to God remains the same. I bet He's even shouting, "I want you!"

So deal a final deathblow to Satan's repetitious lie that you're not worthy. Liberate yourself from the chains of this lie by emphatically declaring, "I don't do this because *I'm* worthy. I do this because *He's* worthy!"

Lie #3: "I don't know enough."

Interesting, isn't it, that eleven of the twelve people Jesus recruited to launch the most important movement in human history were uneducated, ordinary men? And the one educated man betrayed Him. The world impact of these eleven men is irrefutable. Yet not a single record exists of any college diplomas, seminary degrees, or doctorates among them.

Jesus doesn't require any special degrees or knowledge of you, either.

Rather than focusing on what you *don't* know, focus on what you *do* know. You have something far better than *secondhand* information—you have *firsthand* experience. God has given you a compelling story of what He's done in your life. And your story validates that, just like He did in the past, God *still* shows up in people's lives today.

In fact, you undoubtedly possess a whole personal library of God-stories—moments when God has shown up in your life. We always need to learn more about God in His Word, and we need to share it. But His "Word made flesh" in your life—your personal stories—will powerfully impact people and may be just the next step they need.

During the long hours of cross-country road trips in our family car, we often play the alphabet game. It can take awhile to find every letter and eventually arrive at the final winning letter *Z*. Yet you need and appreciate every letter you find along the way. People on a spiritual discovery journey may need "the next letter" *you* have to offer them. It may be a word spoken, an act of kindness, a Spirit-prompted thought you share, or an action God leads you to take.

Whatever God's Spirit prompts you to do or say—trust in Him. However small it seems to you, it may be just the right "next letter needed" in their spiritual search. Forcing yourself or others into pushy or contrived "A to Z" conversations because you think that's what you should do actually may be insensitive overload for them and an expression of low personal trust in the voice of God's Spirit. God needs your willingness to simply be His timely delivery of "the next letter"—helping other people get one more letter further along in their discovery of God's love and plans for them.

A seasoned New Zealand missionary told me, "When a soccer game is won, everyone celebrates the ball's arrival in the goal—but there were a whole lot of feet kicking the ball in the right direction all the way down the field. It takes all the players moving the ball forward—a little or a lot—all the way to the goal. At just the right moment one player enjoys the privilege of putting the ball in the back of the net. It took a team."

Just because some people may know more about God or ministry than you doesn't disqualify you from offering (and using) what you already know to help others get closer to the goal God has for them.

Years ago, the nineteenth-century itinerant evangelist D. L. Moody appeared at an Oxford University chapel service. Not long after he started preaching, his poor grammar began annoying the students. Didn't he know better? Every time he made a grammatical error, the students stomped their feet on the floor. Some say that the chapel service featured more stomping than preaching.

Afterward, a student approached Moody and offered to give him a list of all the grammatical mistakes he made that night.

Although Moody could have apologized or reacted with embarrassment, he refused to allow his lack of formal education to discourage him. Instead, he replied to the student, "I'm *using* all the grammar *I* know to the glory of God. Are you *using* all the grammar *you* know to the glory of God?"

Moody's question applies to us as well. Rather than asking yourself "How much do I know about God?" ask yourself "Am I using what I know about God for His glory and for the good of others?"

God doesn't call us to be information brokers. He calls us to love Him with everything that's within us and then to love people. More than knowledge, love changes lives. And anyone can love.

Let *love* be your legacy, just as it was Christ's (Ephesians 5:1–2).

Your competence comes from God (2 Corinthians 3:4–6). And He always leads you in triumphal procession in Christ and through you spreads everywhere the fragrance of the knowledge of Him (2 Corinthians 2:14).

So get over what you don't know, and give people the delightful aroma of Jesus!

Get In

Charles Blondin, the great nineteenth-century tightrope artist, used to draw crowds by crossing the Niagara River—just downstream from the Falls. He enjoyed terrifying the onlookers with his theatrics.

Sometimes he crossed the river blindfolded; other times he crossed on stilts or with a man on his back.

One time, he stood before the crowd and asked if they believed he could roll a wheelbarrow on the tightrope to the other side. A man anxious to see the feat shouted, "Yes, I believe you can!"

The Great Blondin smiled, rolled the wheelbarrow to the tightrope, and then looked directly at the man. "If you believe I can, then get in!"

At some point in our lives, God asks us to step out in faith and get in the wheelbarrow. It's one thing to say to God, "Yes, I believe You can!" But it's completely different to stop listening to Satan's lies and climb in the wheelbarrow—placing your trust and your life in God's hands.

Living as a Plan A Kingdom laborer requires that you continually take new steps of faith. Sometimes God may ask you to venture outside of your comfort zone—way outside. Sometimes, He may want you to alter little things in the course of an ordinary day. Other times He may ask you to do what seems impossible. If you're unwilling to trust Him, you'll likely drift back to the sidelines, where it's safe and comfortable.

And you'll never experience the incredible joy that awaits those who get in.

In Genesis 12, God told Abram to leave behind his safe life—his country, his people, and his father's household—and embrace the uncertainty of an unknown journey ahead. And Abram obeyed. He didn't know where God was leading him, but he left anyhow. God called him to get in, and he did. Ripples from his "I'm in" decision went further than he ever could have imagined.

At times, living a Plan A life may require that you exchange personal safety, security, and comfort for a moment—or a lifetime—of uncertainty. It requires that you *go* somewhere, *do* something, or *give* something that seems illogical or impractical from a human standpoint. It requires that you get in, just like it did with Abram.

Countless men and women of faith before you have overcome their fears, frailties, and mental roadblocks to take part in God's plan.

Now it's your turn.

It's time to get in.

All in.

Part Four

THE POSSIBILITIES

The potential impact of one Kingdom laborer is incredible. Imagine what could happen if more and more laborers around the world fulfilled their personal role in God's Plan A.

Seventeen
One … Multiplied!

Before reading this chapter, grab a pen and write down the names of five people who have made the greatest impacts on your life. We'll come back to your list later.

In my early days of ministry, I spent six weeks at a language school in Honduras. I hoped it would help me learn Spanish more quickly, a skill I would need in the future when ministering in Spanish-speaking countries.

For part of my experience, arrangements were made for me to live in a Honduran home, where I could practice my conversational Spanish skills with a host family. While living with them, I shared a room containing two twin beds with the fifteen-year-old son, Eduardo.

Speaking Spanish nearly every moment of every day for weeks on end was pretty intense. Fortunately, the slower pace of life than what I knew back in the States gave Eduardo and me plenty of time to hang out—sometimes stretching an introvert like me.

Before I arrived, I looked forward to spending lots of time alone—a luxury I rarely experienced back home. Eduardo, on the other hand, was looking forward to spending lots of time with this new "big brother."

One of the first mornings, I woke up early to spend some time alone with God. I read my Bible and prayed as quietly as possible, so I wouldn't wake up my roommate. But Eduardo soon woke up and noticed I wasn't in my bed.

"What are you doing?" he asked.

"I'm spending time *alone* with God," I replied, emphasizing the *alone* part.

"Can I join you?"

After hesitating for a moment, I felt God prompting me to welcome Eduardo into my quiet time. Later, He prompted me to fully welcome my new "younger brother" into my life as well.

Eduardo joined me that morning and nearly every morning for the next six weeks. We read the Bible together, and he asked a lot of questions. We prayed together and talked about many aspects of our spiritual lives.

As time passed, it became increasingly clear to me that God had connected our lives for a reason. But He didn't bring us together just so I could impact Eduardo's life. God used Eduardo to impact my life as well.

Eduardo's relationship with God grew much deeper that summer, and the trajectory of his life changed forever. And, in a way, so did mine.

As I lived up close to Eduardo's life and spiritually invested in him, I began to understand and appreciate why Jesus ministered in such a one-on-one relational way.

That summer, I assumed God sent me to Honduras to learn Spanish—and spending time with Eduardo was a side benefit. Now I think it was the other way around. Yes, my Spanish improved during my stay, but I think God sent me to Honduras to spend six weeks with Eduardo.

Ironically, I haven't used my Spanish skills as much as I'd hoped. But Eduardo and I have stayed in contact ever since. I helped him attend a Christian summer youth camp the following year, and I later helped him attend a Christian university in the United States—all the while, connecting him with peers who could help him continue growing in his faith.

His younger sister Mimi later followed him to the United States and attended the same Christian university, where she grew in her faith and met her husband.

Eduardo returned to Honduras after college, and today he disciples young people in the capital city of Tegucigalpa.

He hangs out with students in the public schools during lunch, helping them grow stronger in their relationship with Jesus by investing in their lives what others have invested into his. He prays and studies the Bible with them and talks with them about their walks with God.

Just like I did with him years ago—for a short, but God-appointed time.

A few years ago, I spoke with Eduardo on the phone. At one point in our conversation, he said, "Dwight, I'm doing for others what you did for me—because my spiritual condition would be much different if we hadn't spent those six weeks together."

In that special moment I saw more clearly the importance of that time, and I imagined that some time in the future, one of "his kids" would say the same thing to him.

Spiritual Multiplication

While on earth, Jesus gave us a highly relational model for developing and growing people. It included treating His disciples as friends.

He ate with His disciples around meal tables. He walked and

talked with them on long journeys and camped with them in remote places. He encouraged them, prayed with them, served with them, and ultimately entrusted His eternal cause to them—all in highly relational ways.

By today's quick-addition standards, Jesus' ministry might be judged a failure. He spent a great deal of time hanging out with a relatively small number of disciples—teaching them through His words, actions, and life. His methods didn't seem very time efficient, and early on, His movement didn't sustain much numerical growth.

Maybe that's why few people employ Jesus' methods today.

But through Jesus, God gave us a different kind of ministry strategy—spiritual multiplication. Given enough time, it makes an enduring and powerful impact. The results of Jesus' model prove that the most powerful form of ministry occurs in a relational context—up close over time. That's what Jesus did. And it's what I did with Eduardo during my time in Honduras.

Jesus' ministry model can be summarized in this way: *More time with fewer people equals a greater Kingdom investment.*

This idea plays a critical part in Jesus' Plan A for reaching the world. He's looking for willing laborers who will invest their time in close relationships with other people, organically passing on to them the values of His Kingdom.

Mass Production

Here's the deal, though: As critical as up-close, relational ministry is to Jesus' Plan A, it runs contrary to today's values and fails to measure up to the logic that society has instilled in us since we were young. It's countercultural. In fact, it's even counterintuitive for most of us.

Societal and business plans run on the logic of efficiency and cost-effective mass production. In other words, the goal is to reach (or sell, or convince) the greatest number of people for the least amount of money and time. But God's Plan A runs on the logic of one-life-at-a-time investments in others—a slower, seemingly inefficient, relational process. A process that rarely yields *quick,* tangible results.

I must confess, God's ministry strategy can be a tough sell—even among Christians—because the mass-production mind-set has woven itself into the fabric of our daily lives. We can't escape it.

Today, nearly every product is mass-produced in manufacturing plants. Long gone are the days of artistically handcrafted furniture, hand-stitched and tailor-fit clothing, and homegrown, homemade meals raised or harvested from the family farm. The Industrial Revolution changed all that.

As a society, we believe that mass production provides the best and most efficient way to accomplish nearly everything.

But as efficient and cost effective as it may be, it *doesn't* provide the best model for people-oriented activities … like spiritual development. Our spiritual lives cannot be mass-produced. Nor can relationships.

Which leads me to an important observation: Kingdom laborers cannot be mass-produced.

Maybe that's why God chose to express His love for the world in the form of *a person*—His Son, Jesus, the Word who became flesh. And maybe that's why in Jesus' three short years of recorded ministry, His most effective ministry occurred in life-on-life encounters and relationships, rather than in large-venue events.

Still, our modern-day mind-set for ministry prescribes that speaking to massive crowds and televising programs to as many people as possible are the best ways to reach the world for Christ. While these approaches—which work on the rules of addition—may reach more people in the short run, they actually reach fewer people in the long run. And they reach them less effectively than relational ministry. Our goal of multiplied Plan A Kingdom laborers requires an "ancient future" unearthing of Jesus' ministry strategy.

Do the Math

Jesus based His relational ministry model on the rules of multiplication. For that reason, some have said Jesus' vision involved "spiritual multiplication." Jesus staked the future of the Kingdom on passing His values and truths through His personal relationships with some ordinary guys. He told them to do the same.

But somewhere along the way we lost track of His method. A rediscovery of its vast potential requires only a calculator and some simple math.

If you spoke to one hundred thousand people each year for the next twenty years (an overly ambitious goal even for public speakers), you would reach *two million people*. That's simple addition. That also assumes you have no fear of public speaking.

But if you regularly invested yourself in the lives of two different people each year (a very attainable number) for the next twenty years—and you charged both of them to pour their lives into two more people each year (who would do the same, and so on)—you would, together, reach most of the world's population. That's "spiritual multiplication"—Jesus-style.

Year	Public Speaking (+)	Life-on-Life Investing (x)
1	100,000	2
2	200,000	8
5	500,000	242
10	1,000,000	59,048
15	1,500,000	14,348,906
20	2,000,000	3,486,784,400

Obviously, the math wouldn't play out quite this perfectly as some attrition would occur (like Jesus experienced with Judas), but you get the point: Over time, spiritual multiplication is a powerful strategy for reaching the world. In fact, it's the only strategy that could possibly reach a world of more than six billion people.

Following in Jesus' footsteps, the apostle Paul charged Timothy to invest his life in and entrust spiritual truths to "reliable men who will also be qualified to teach others" (2 Timothy 2:2).

An ancient legend tells the story of an emperor of China who loved playing the game of checkers. So, he summoned the man who invented the game and asked him to be his guest of honor at a regal banquet, with other dignitaries in attendance. At the end of the dinner, the emperor asked the man, "Make any request, and I will grant it to you."

Burdened for hungry people in India, he decided to take advantage of the exponential power of multiplication and compounding.

"If it please you, give me one grain of wheat for the first square of my checkerboard, two grains for the second square, four for the third square, eight for the fourth square, sixteen for the fifth square, and so on until my entire checkerboard has been accounted for."

Insulted by such a "meager" request, the emperor demanded that the man be thrown out of his presence. But the emperor failed to realize that the outrageous request would cover the entire country of India in one foot of grain!

That's the power of multiplication.

And that same power applies when we invest in the life of one person who then invests in the life of another. What seems small at first multiplies exponentially over time!

The Key to Making Deep Impact

Spiritual multiplication not only reaches more people over time but also impacts lives in deeper ways.

In other words, it's a ministry strategy that is both deep and wide. Now let's apply this to your life.

At the beginning of this chapter, I asked you to write down the names of five people who made the greatest impact on you.

1. How many of the names on your list are people with whom you've had a close relationship?

2. How many of the names are speakers, authors, or others with whom you've had little or no relationship?

When I pose these questions to individuals or groups, more than 80 percent answer that their greatest influences resulted from meaningful, up-close relationships. That's the power of up-close time and influence.

As founding president of a speaking ministry, I witness firsthand the deep impact God makes in people's lives through our speakers. People respond by the tens, hundreds, and thousands—making life-changing decisions. At our Kingdom Building Ministries (KBM) headquarters, we continually receive calls, letters, and emails from people worldwide, living out their decisions many years later.

But despite the impact of these significant decisions at our events, our speakers and staff believe nothing can replace the power of one life pouring into another over time in the context of a relationship.

Nothing.

Kingdom laborers are produced through life-on-life transfer. Think about it: Jesus preached powerful sermons to "the multitudes," but He spent most of His time investing in the lives of a small group of individuals. We see little lasting legacy effect from people who heard Jesus speak, but we see lasting Kingdom impact—a movement—spawned by a small few who spent up-close relational time with Him.

When we pass on the values and priorities of the Kingdom, far more is "caught" than "taught." We raise our biological children this way—and Kingdom laborers are best raised this way too.

The disciples benefited by *seeing* Jesus in different kinds of settings—*seeing* Him model His passionate love for God and people in the context of everyday, along-the-way life—with all of its surprises and complications.

And God allows *us* to see the life of Jesus by giving us access to the historic accounts of Jesus' life in the Gospels. God blessed us with Jesus' teachings, the red-letter words in the Gospels. But He also gave us the stories about Jesus' life—the black letters—for us to also see how He lived.

You, too, will make the greatest impact on people who live, work, play, and do life in close proximity to you. God designed it that way. And it's how Jesus modeled it—using all of life as a classroom.

Your Job Description in Spiritual Multiplication

You may have some concerns about multiplying yourself, because you don't want to pass on your shortcomings to others. But spiritual multiplication is not about multiplying *yourself.* It's about multiplying followers of *Jesus*.

Your job description in multiplying followers of Jesus isn't complicated, and it doesn't require extraordinary gifts. Here it is:

> Prayer (Acts 1:14)
>
> Tons of encouragement (Hebrews 3:13)
>
> Humility (Philippians 2:3–4)
>
> Dedication to memorizing Scripture together (Joshua 1:8)
>
> Continually passing on to others everything you can think of that's helped you grow in your walk with God (2 Timothy 2:2)
>
> Meeting on a regular basis (Hebrews 10:24–25)

Basically, your job description is to come alongside others in their spiritual journeys and help them set (and keep) their gazes on Jesus—the Author and Perfecter of *their* faith (Hebrews 12:2).

Any follower of Jesus can do that!

Some fear that they don't know enough to help other laborers mature in their faith. But you don't need to know all the answers—if you know the One who does. So instead of offering pat answers, why not lay down your ego and join them on a journey of praying and seeking answers together? You'll both grow faster and go farther.

The testimony of Dawson Trotman, the founder of the Navigators, profoundly impacted my life. He often asked, "Where's your man? Where is your woman?" In other words, "Who are you helping to explore and discover God's Word and His plan for their lives?"

Jesus did ministry one life at a time. And He's calling you to do the same.

A Postscript

Recently, I traveled with some of our KBM speakers throughout El Salvador, visiting Compassion International's child-development centers and partner churches. We also spent time in the homes of impoverished families, listening to them share how Compassion International had affected their lives.

Our home visits had the greatest impact on me, especially my visit with one family. Halfway through the trip, I visited the home of the family whose child we sponsor, Wilbert.

Traveling on the bumpy dirt roads to their home, I felt as if I were about to burst with anticipation and excitement. Finally, we arrived at the house where I met Wilbert, his parents, and the rest of his family. For the next unforgettable hour, I began building a relationship with this family in their world. Before leaving, I gave

Wilbert and his parents gifts from our family, encouraged them, and prayed with them. And as I left, I pledged that this was just the beginning of a lifelong relationship.

The next morning at breakfast in our Salvadoran hotel, I sat next to our Compassion tour guide, Rocio.

"How was your experience yesterday when you met your sponsor child?" she asked.

"I'm overwhelmed with excitement!" I answered.

She smiled warmly and asked, "What was most exciting about it?"

"Well, this may sound strange, but what excited me most was seeing little Wilbert's life through a visionary lens." Rocio gave me a confused look, so I explained what I meant. "As I stood in his home, I could 'see' beyond this season of his life to what God might do in him and through him in the future. I know other people with me yesterday saw a little six-year-old boy. But I saw a grown man serving God and impacting the lives of others some day."

"Wow, that *is* a different perspective," Rocio responded. "What caused you to see him in that visionary way?"

"Well, many years ago, when I attended a language school in Honduras, God allowed me to build a relationship with a young Honduran boy whose life has become an amazing testimony of God's power and purpose."

Rocio's warm expression quickly changed to shock. She put her hands over her face and started weeping.

For a moment, I wasn't sure how to interpret her response.

"Oh my word, you're talking about Eduardo, aren't you?" she exclaimed.

Now *I* looked shocked. I couldn't believe it. How did she know who I was talking about?

Confused and amazed, I asked, "Rocio, how would you possibly know Eduardo?"

"He's my cousin!" she replied. And then through swells of tearful emotion, she went on to tell me Eduardo's story from her perspective.

"For many years, my mother and I have wondered how Eduardo developed such a mature love for God and how he's had such a profound spiritual influence on others. We wondered how this could've happened when his own father never had a personal relationship with God."

Now *I* was on the verge of tears.

"Dwight, one time I asked him about his passion for God. I wanted to know how such an ordinary kid had become such an extraordinary servant of God. He told me that God had placed an American man in his life years ago to spark his spiritual passion. Oh my word, *you* are that man he was talking about, aren't you? I can't believe it! I can't believe it! I'm in total shock!"

And quite honestly, I was in shock too.

Why did God orchestrate such a revelatory, impromptu encounter with Rocio at the same time I was writing this book? Was it to speak to Rocio about how God multiplies our seemingly insignificant life-on-life ministry efforts? Was it to encourage me to keep on pouring into the lives of other future Kingdom laborers like Eduardo?

Or was this postscript intended by God to benefit you? Perhaps God allowed this to happen to put an exclamation point on how He wants to multiply *your* efforts and lead you into giving yourself to others. May I ask …

Who is *your* Eduardo?

Eighteen
Passing the Baton

When Dara was in third grade, I enjoyed watching her participate with her classmates in their end-of-the-year field-day events—a sack race, tug-of-war, hundred-yard dash, and other games. The final—and funniest—event of the day ended up being the relay race. Each class chose a four-person team featuring its best runners to compete in the event.

Dara glanced over at me with great pride when she found out she was going to run on her class's team. I gave her a thumbs-up and then instinctively sized up the other teams to determine which one had the best chance to win. I quickly concluded Dara's team was the odds-on favorite (of course!).

The gym teacher held up the baton and explained its importance to all of the participants. He said that the relay is a team event and that the baton links the team together. Each runner would begin by running to the end of the field, turn around, and then run back with the baton in his or her hand.

"But," he said, "the next runner may not run before receiving the baton."

"Any runner who starts running without the baton will be disqualified!" he barked in his gruff gym-teacher voice.

Within moments, he called out the starting cadence: "On your mark … get set … go!"

The runners lunged forward, but it didn't take long for a few of them to surge ahead of the pack. Dara's teammate Courtney led the miniature army of runners. At the end of the field, she headed back toward her teammates, well ahead of her competitors.

But what happened next both stunned and amused the crowd.

Courtney ran so fast and with such intent focus on what she mistakenly believed was the finish line that she ran right past her teammates standing on the starting line … with the baton still in her hand. She ran her leg of the race with such enthusiasm and speed that she completely forgot that her fellow runners needed the baton in order to begin their legs of the race. It was a relay. She had teammates.

And she forgot their need for the baton!

Courtney's teammates (and tons of parents, too) tried to get her attention, but she was entrenched in her own world.

"Come back! Bring back the baton! We're going to lose!" the cries rose.

Finally, the next runner on the team chased Courtney down, yanked the baton out of her hand, and desperately pursued the second-to-last runner in an all-out effort to get her team back in the race.

But oddly enough, the frenzy of the race and her singular focus diverted the girl's attention, and *she* forgot to pass the baton to Dara at the end of her leg too!

Despite their great relay potential, Dara's team didn't win the race—or even come close.

However, they *did* provide a vivid picture of how important passing the baton is.

The Successful Exchange

That field-day relay debacle reminded me of the importance of passing the baton in the Kingdom of God. No wonder the Kingdom suffers from a severe shortage of Plan A laborers, shallow spiritual depth, and far more consumers than contributors. Not enough people are imitating Jesus and passing the baton.

Numerous people have confided in me, stating that they feel stuck in "spiritual childhood" because no one passed the spiritual baton to them. Too often we have emphasized "reaching" over "teaching." We have spent time and money on worthy evangelistic outreaches but neglected the time-consuming process of Kingdom baton passing.

Although God expects us to run on His team, few people have been equipped to run in such a way as to get the prize (1 Corinthians 9:24). And it's not their fault. You can't fault a baby for failing to develop into a high-functioning adult without parents who love, nurture, and model to the child what it means to grow up.

As a matter of fact, high-functioning teens and young adults usually have parents beside and behind them continually passing on to them what is most important. Yet God's Kingdom falters from an absence of spiritual maturity and the lack of understanding about Kingdom laborership. While filled with potential, we lack the nurture required to develop. Too many needy and deserving people wait for someone—anyone—to come alongside and pass to them what will transform their Plan A potential into reality.

Passing the baton isn't foreign to our experience. We see it modeled when work supervisors mentor their young employees, when devoted coaches spend extra time instructing their young athletes, when teachers pass insights to their students, or when parents devote themselves to imparting key values and important life skills to their children. Whenever this baton passing occurs, it pays big dividends in the next generation!

Likewise, Kingdom laborers who not only run their *own* legs of the race with perseverance but also devote themselves to *passing batons* to other runners make all the difference! Unfortunately, this rarely takes place.

Perhaps we haven't clearly understood the anatomy of a successful baton pass.

The Q & As of a Successful Baton Pass

As I witnessed Dara's field day, I realized passing the baton doesn't just happen. It requires intentionality and teamwork. Because successful coaching (and baton passing) flourishes in a climate of dialogue, I'll describe a successful baton pass through a series of questions and answers:

> Q: What is the baton?
>
> A: "The baton" is the spiritual wealth God has given you, which can help other people near you function with greater influence, spiritual energy, strength, confidence, fervor, focus, knowledge, or speed.
>
> Q: Who should I pass the baton to?
>
> A: God will prompt you as you seek His guidance (see chapter 14). He knows what you have to offer and who needs it most. Baton-passing relationships work best when the two people are of the same gender. The "receiver" must be reliable (2 Timothy 2:2), hungry for God and His truth,

demonstrate a teachable spirit, show respect for you, and desire to live a God-pleasing life of spiritual obedience and influence.

Q: What does it mean to pass the baton?

A: Passing the baton means freely sharing your spiritual wealth with others. Any time you share what God has taught you, how He's encouraged you, or allowed you to learn from others—and you share it with people for their spiritual growth and Plan A living—you are *baton passing*. It usually occurs in the context of relationships, so it develops organically (informally) rather than systematically (formally).

Q: When do I pass the baton?

A: When you live and train as a Plan A runner on God's "relay team," you see runners everywhere to whom you can pass the baton. Be aware that they may pass a baton to you as well. But as you actively seek out other runners, you will discover endless opportunities to talk, pray, encourage, bless, and pass everything you can to them.

Q: Can I pass thc baton?

A: If you assume you have very little to offer, you may be equating passing the baton with an information brain

> dump. But the best passers are people with practical tips that come from real-life experience. Earlier in the race you received help from God and others. Even though you're learning more with each stride, you've watched others run a strong race.
>
> Q: What does passing the baton look like?
>
> A: Your passing skills will develop as you become a student of your "Eduardo's" life and as you learn to recognize his or her strengths and weaknesses.
>
> Pray with them and for them. Ask God to grow in your heart His love for them. Affirm their strengths every way you can—speak of them out loud, in print, in front of others—and when you pray with them, thank God for His plans to further His Kingdom through them. Ask God to reveal their weak areas and then to help you discern the best way to speak the truth *in love* (Ephesians 4:15). Seek God's continual presence and help in the process of this delicate soul surgery.

I love the way Larry Crabb conveys this idea in his important book *Connecting:*

> When I sense that you want to discover what's wrong with me and change me, I will either slide into passivity ("Go ahead! Fix me!") or raise myself up to an arrogant height

> ("I can handle things. I'll consider what you say, but I'll make sure I don't buy all of it!"). But when I know that you love me, that you believe in me, that you recognize something terrific in me, that you long to see my potential released, I'm more inclined to receive you and let you pour into my life.[†]

We trust people who delight in us, who see the good beneath the bad and call out the good. (Visit www.KBM.org for a list of practical baton-passing tips.)

It's Your Turn

Imagine that you're a part of a relay team. The runner before you has placed the baton in your hand. Now it's your turn.

You begin running your leg of the race as swiftly as you can. You stumble here and there, but you keep getting up. You know that all runners stumble from time to time in *this* race.

You round the corner of the track, and you see a teammate with an outstretched arm standing before you. The runner's gaze is fixed ahead as you begin your approach.

What will you do?

Don't hesitate.

Go ahead. With God's Spirit helping you, pass your baton.

Endnote

[†] Larry Crabb, *Connecting* (Nashville, TN: Word Publishing, 1997), 70.

Nineteen
Almost Missing It

I seldom sleep on flights. But boarding my late-night flight from Washington, D.C., back to Denver, I was exhausted following a weekend of ministry. Flight attendants immediately passed out pillows and blankets in full expectation that most of us would sleep in the hours ahead.

As soon as the plane took off, I reclined my seat and squirmed around until I found a somewhat comfortable position. Almost immediately I began to doze off.

I'm not sure how much time had passed when a passenger across the aisle put his hand on my shoulder and startled me out of my deep sleep.

Abruptly waking in a strange place with a strange man hovering over me, I nearly came up swinging!

The man realized his quick need to explain.

"Sir, I'm sorry to wake you up, but you've gotta look out of the window on my side of the plane."

"Is something wrong?" I interrupted, still in a state of startled panic.

"No, not at all," he replied. "It's just that there's the most incredible lightning show going on in the sky on this side of the plane. I've never seen anything like it. I think you'll want to see it."

His excited invitation failed to convince me that whatever was happening on his side of the airplane was worth interrupting my sleep. As a frequent flier, I have witnessed plenty of heavenly power-and-light shows from airplane windows over the years. Really good ones. On this night, I didn't need to see a lightning show. I needed to sleep.

I sat for a moment, a little upset. But I knew I wouldn't be able to get back to sleep.

The man must have felt my resistance.

"Sir, it's really spectacular. You should see it."

The half-empty plane made it easy to slide over to his side and look out the window.

What I witnessed next was truly amazing—a once-in-a-lifetime experience. I've never seen anything like it before or since. Nearly every second, a new lightning bolt fired and created a new color and light pattern in the cumulus clouds. And my reaction resembled his.

"Wow! I've never seen anything like it! It's amazing!" I said in a voice far too loud for the dark, sleepy environment of the plane's cabin.

I quickly turned around to see if I'd wakened anyone. Several sleep-disturbed faces glared back at me.

Suddenly, I became the insensitive guy who woke me up. But now I understood. I repeated to the others what the guy said to me. Initially, they looked just as annoyed as I had moments earlier.

"I'm sorry to wake you, but I've traveled for years, and something amazing is happening in the sky on this side of the plane." I wanted them to enjoy it with me—and I was convinced they would eventually appreciate my insistence once they witnessed the same majestic heavenly production as my new friend and me.

A bit reluctantly, a few other passengers made their way to the windows, suddenly responding like me.

Before I knew it, our reaction to the lightning storm started a slow domino effect throughout the plane. One person after another heard the stirring commotion and watched the growing crowd peering out the windows on one side of the plane. Soon, nearly everyone in the plane—including the flight attendants—joined us, watching the incredible "fireworks" display. The ever-increasing volume of "oohs" and "aahs" in the once-sleepy environment made for a humorous scene.

Only minutes before, nearly all of us were asleep. Suddenly, we were wide awake and fully engaged. And it all started with just one guy committed to waking us up before we missed our fleeting once-in-a-lifetime opportunity.

Once the show ended, I thanked the fellow near me for waking me. I assured him that I was glad he took the risk because he gave me—and all the others—the experience of a lifetime. He told me he was glad he did it.

Awakening the Sleeping Giant

In the World War II movies *Tora! Tora! Tora!* and *Pearl Harbor,* Japanese Admiral Isoroku Yamamoto supposedly remarked to his fleet after they attacked Pearl Harbor, "I fear all we have done is to awaken a sleeping giant and fill him with a terrible resolve."

If Yamamoto really said this line or even thought it, he was correct.

Before the attack, the United States was content watching the war—despite having the power and human resources necessary to influence its outcome.

The war seemed so far away, so removed from the daily lives of everyday Americans. But when the Japanese surprised the United States in their attack on Pearl Harbor, they awakened the "sleeping giant," brought it to its feet, and filled it with great resolve.

For too long, the body of Christ has played the sleeping giant! The time has come for Kingdom laborers to jostle and wake up their fellow passengers from their slumber so they won't miss their once-in-a-lifetime opportunity.

So how do we awaken this incredibly massive and potential-laden sleeping giant? What will it take to fill Christ's worldwide body with great resolve?

Imagine if all Christians "woke up from their slumber," apart from the two hours they go to church every week, and fully engaged in God's Plan A for their lives the additional 166 hours. They wouldn't quit their jobs, but they would see their jobs differently, their relationships differently, their lives differently. If they fully engaged themselves the other 166 hours in God's Plan A for their lives, imagine the manpower! The new Kingdom exploits! The possibilities all around us! Imagine this resurrection power awakening God's army of everyday people worldwide! That's a massive "sleeping giant" bigger than Yamamoto's greatest fear. It's worth awakening, one person at a time!

The future of God's Kingdom lies in human resources.

It begins with you and me—and every Christian—waking up to our everyday calling as Kingdom laborers.

Then we must awaken the sleeping giant—using whatever grass-roots influence we have, joining others who are virally spreading a wildfire Plan A movement—one life at a time, domino-style!

Imagine if *every* Christian worldwide woke up and reported for duty!

You can help spread the movement. Like the early followers of Jesus who announced His life-changing resurrection person to person, you can share His life, hope, power, and presence everywhere.

This movement will spread as we become so deeply convinced of the power of God's Plan A for our lives that we tell others who tell others who tell others—until the swelling tide of influence makes the much-needed change. You can do your part in awakening the sleeping giant in the following ways:

> *Surrender your 24/7 life to Him.* Offer your life as a living sacrifice for Spirit-directed service in His Kingdom.
>
> *Pursue God's Plan A for your life.* Live your everyday life as a Kingdom laborer, making yourself available as God's up-close, along-the-way, mainstream, in-the-moment, camouflaged, storytelling, love-the-one-in-front-of-you minister in your sphere of influence.
>
> *Pass the baton.* This is key: Like the runner on a relay team, don't just run the race marked out for yourself—pass the baton of these Plan A truths to others. Pass them a copy of this book. Consider going through the questions online at www.DavidCCook.com/PlanA with someone special or with a small group of friends. Pray that God will lead you to others—even perfect strangers—who may need to be woken up and jump-started as potential Plan A laborers. Multiply yourself in as many ways as you can think of. As you awaken others, they will wake up yet others, until

> your influence will stretch farther than you ever imagined. And the Lord of the harvest will send every new Kingdom laborer into a new spiritual harvest field of influence.

There's a plane full of people sleeping through the most important and exciting season of spiritual history. Who are you going to wake up first?

Epilogue
Imagine

The pastor stood at the front of the large church sanctuary, anointed Kara with oil, and commissioned her in prayer as she prepared to return to the mission field.

As the pastor prayed, my mind flashed back to the slide presentations I watched as a child when missionaries from around the world visited our church. They intrigued me, but I never really understood what they did or why they did it.

In some ways, this commissioning service resembled all the others I had seen before. The pastor truly believed that our church was playing an important sending role in Kara's ministry. He had repeated that idea several times.

But in other ways, this commissioning service differed greatly from the others I'd seen in the past.

You see, Kara is not an overseas missionary. She's a mother of five whose primary place of ministry is in a suburban neighborhood about twenty miles away.

If you ask her what she does, she'll tell you she's a stay-at-home mom. If you ask her the location of her mission field, she'll say that sometimes it's in her neighborhood, at the park, the community pool, or her kids' schools or athletic fields.

This commissioning service differed in another way as well. Kara was not the only one commissioned that Sunday. John, a company president, was being commissioned. So were Nate and Christy, who manage a large apartment complex. An elderly man who mentors young students each year for a local school came forward as well. All over the sanctuary, Plan A Kingdom laborers were consecrating themselves to God's everyday service, receiving anointing and commissioning prayers from pastors and elders of the church. It was so moving.

By the end of the morning, thousands of laborers were anointed with oil and commissioned like Kara. The masses of people of different ages and from all walks of life were being sent outside the walls into the harvest fields of spiritual influence everywhere. What a powerful scene to behold.

The pastor and church leaders clearly validated the unique ministry of every single laborer, sending them to "be the church"—Christ's body, up close.

But that's not all they communicated. In the same symbolic act, they conveyed how powerful and pervasive a force the body of Christ could be if every Christian fulfilled God's Plan A as an everyday Kingdom laborer in every facet and sphere of society.

As I watched church leaders anointing these laborers at various stations around the sanctuary, I began asking myself some compelling questions.

What would happen if churches around the world challenged, equipped, commissioned, and sent their attendees into the world as active Kingdom laborers?

What if people like James the Roofer, Grace the Grandma, Bruce the Businessman, and Lance the Student felt valued, endorsed, empowered, and sent out to more fully minister and serve in their mainstream places of influence?

What if people and churches everywhere began to reclaim and revive Jesus' plan?

What if the body of Christ shook off their shackles of previous unemployment in Christ's Kingdom, stepped up, and reported for duty?

What if churches all over the world held commissioning services like this one?

What if we made time during our weekly worship gatherings for people to give a "Body of Christ Report," bearing witness to God's activities in their companies, schools, factories, neighborhoods, coffee shops, parks, and anywhere they are being God's love-in-the-middle, everyday laborers?

God sparked something in me as my imagination ran wild. This life-changing experience gave birth to a fervent prayer and a cause worthy of my life … and yours.

Imagine: The Holy Spirit blowing off the dust of a two-thousand-year-old plan, restoring it, and raising it to life in our generation.

Imagine: You and I receiving and then living out God's Plan A for our lives, and then touching thousands, and then millions, with hearts on fire and lives devoted to Him.

The world will never be the same.

Oh Lord, may it be!

Acknowledgments

As a young boy, people called me "Dwight the Fright." On most days, my nickname was well deserved. But God's love changed everything. He pursued and eventually convinced me that the One who knew me best actually loved me most. It changed my life!

But difficult relational circumstances later tested my faith. Hurt and disappointment almost derailed me. Then a godly man commented to me, "Dwight, God never told you to look at any man. He said to 'fix your eyes on Jesus.'" From that day forward I lifted my gaze. Jesus became my model, hero, friend, and Rock of whom it is written, "The one who trusts in him will never be put to shame" (Romans 9:33). Looking to Jesus and pointing to Jesus are my goals. The world needs Him—not me. I'm the delivery boy charged with dispensing His love, ways, and presence to people in their everyday world.

So, Jesus is the message of this book. He is our only model to follow, our Plan A quintessential trail guide to "live a life of love" (Ephesians 5:1–2) just like He did.

Jesus deployed His early disciples in twos—demonstrating that Kingdom building is largely a "co-laborership" enterprise. Similarly, this book has involved others whom I consider my "co-laborers."

Without question, first on my list is my wife, Dawn—my lover and best friend. Our heart-locked journey is a joint venture in loving God and others. Into my intense life, Dawn brings joy, love, laughter, fun, and beauty. My retreat, confidante, and closest ally, she was tailored for me by God in seemingly every matter. Because her prayers are powerful, her grace endless, and her conviction to follow God's will fervent and strong, my life and this book come to you nurtured by her. She lives with Dwight the Fright, yet loves me as though I am Dwight the Great. I could have never imagined receiving such love, healing hugs, or life camaraderie. I am blessed beyond what I deserve!

Dara and Dreyson, my daughter and son, make parenting the easiest, most rewarding experience I've ever known. They've definitely made me a better person. While marriage may produce a master's degree in life, parenting must be God's strategy for a doctorate. I've learned tons from my kids! We openly love, talk, and pray together. I can't imagine two kids blessing, praying, or sacrificing more for this book to be in your hands. I'm so proud of them. Dara (my "favorite princess") and Dreyson (my "best bud") are incessant God-lovers and my truly amazing co-laborers. We're a team!

Throughout their lives, my remarkable parents, Dave and Agnes, have modeled how living a "life of love" can affect so many people. In every community and neighborhood they've lived, they leave behind a trail of love. Rather than make greatness their pursuit, they endeavor to live as servants of a great God. I'm so proud of my folks. I'm also grateful for how they loved a mess in process and encouraged me further than my eyes could see. They're still going strong in their retirement years—loving, modeling, and serving as co-laborers in this book's message and the ministry behind it.

I've also been hugely blessed by a patient, gracious, loving, and supportive extended family—on both sides of our marriage. They amaze me! I'm undeserving of their great love, their ongoing and uplifting "family blessing," and their unswerving Kingdom devotion as co-laborers in Christ's cause.

For many years, God provided a special ministry co-laborer from a church I once pastored. This special friend eventually came alongside my early ministry efforts, first as a volunteer and later as a dear staff member. Through our years together, Mark Vermilion acquired an ability to "get" me and understand the heart of my Plan A message and ministry calling. I am forever thankful for this God-sent partner who brought my heart, my ministry-oration style, and my messages to print.

Recently God brought writer Michael J. Klassen alongside me to help turn this book into reality. Michael is a gifted writer and a man of God with a heart that resonates with mine. What an extraordinary pleasure to work through the pages of this book with him.

Susan Tjaden, an amazing editor, and the David C. Cook team have been wonderful co-laborers—highly committed to strengthen, bless, and deliver God's Plan A message. We share a common Kingdom mind-set!

I cannot imagine a finer literary agent than Andrew Wolgemuth of Wolgemuth & Associates. God must be pleased with this godly, humble, and highly professional servant. I certainly am.

Twenty years ago, a vivacious young woman with a heart after God approached me following a speaking engagement. Little did I know that she would eventually become the publicist for me and this book. Lesley Burbridge of Rogers & Cowan is an exceptional Kingdom co-laborer.

The book you hold in your hands has been saturated in prayer by a team of incredible people with whom I communicate often—my co-laboring "Personal Prayer Partners." I consider them to be some of God's finest servants! They faithfully pray Kingdom-advancing, difference-making prayers. Through their prayers, they bring God's plans, purposes, and power to earth. They've earnestly prayed for you, expecting the Holy Spirit of God to meet with you and to transform your life and future through these pages. You've been earnestly covered in prayer by this incredible team of intercessors.

In 1986, Kingdom Building Ministries began with a call from God to raise up laborers—people who would passionately and actively love God and others with "hearts on fire and lives on purpose." The vision was daunting, but God promised us, "I will call others, and together you will do it." Since then, many people have helped in countless ways to seek the fulfillment of God's Plan A in our generation.

An extraordinary team of itinerant speakers from KBM has colabored with me for decades, challenging and equipping people to adopt God's values and become His laborers. Past and present KBM office staff and board members have worked tirelessly to extend this mission to the farthest reaches of the earth. Board member Roger Muselman and his wife, Naomi, have helped greatly expand our laborership-message delivery, providing generous amounts of donated printing.

Countless men and women from all walks of life have believed in and supported this message as KBM Investors, Prayer Workers, and Alumni. They've given sacrificially to ensure this message not only reaches your hands, but ultimately impacts your life as well. Some of them so effectively live Plan A lives that their stories have been presented in these pages to better help you see and take hold of God's Plan A for you.

Special encouragers (they know who they are), manuscript-review friends (so helpful to me), and special think-tank friends (Kristian, Brandi, Travis, and Shelley) were all used by God to strengthen this book.

God paraded before me countless people who exemplified the Plan A message—humble men and women of God, unknown and unheralded by this world but no doubt well known in heaven. I'm pretty sure they'll be heaven-shocked one day by what God has prepared for them—something far better than earthly renown.

Other servants of God who influenced me through their life legacies, writings, and special moments together: Lorne Sanny (a reluctant leader who graciously spent time with me), Dawson Trotman (a passionate believer in one-on-one discipleship), Bill Bright (who graciously stopped during a walk with me one day and asked, "How can I *serve* you?"), Robert Coleman (his truth-wielding book *The Master Plan of Evangelism* powerfully changed my life trajectory at age eighteen), Dwight Moody (a true "heart on fire," with God-inspired zeal to not only speak, but also train "lay men and women" to live out their lives ablaze for God around the world), Ann Kiemel (an unintimidating, ordinary single woman in the late 1960s who communicated her message in a unique and irreproducible way to a generation of Christians; her touching stories inspired people to believe that Jesus wanted to use ordinary people to extend His love everywhere), Corrie ten Boom and Joni Eareckson Tada (who demonstrated to me and others that God can redeem some of life's worst tragedies), and Jim Elliot (a young guy who loved people up close and whose short-lived missionary venture resulted in far more than he could have ever imagined. In the wake of his martyrdom, his young widow, Elisabeth, began sharing Jim's life message and spoke at a small-town gathering that I attended when I was just seven years old. God used that night to provoke in me a deep calling of whatever it takes, God's will and His message must go forth).

Finally, rather unique to what's most typical of the life and employment journey of a "minster," I've been blessed by God's sovereign leading and the trust and employment of others to get to learn, test, and apply Plan A principles taught and modeled by Christ in past retail employment, holistic medical-team service, civic boards, community involvement, neighborhood-association boards, and in a wide variety of mainstream relationships, some with perfect "strangers" God led into my path. In all these situations I've discovered mainstream people and places receptive to God's plan.

I'm hopeful you will discover that *you* are God's Plan A … and there is no Plan B!